COMMUNITY, STATE, AND CHURCH

COMMUNITY, STATE, AND CHURCH

Three Essays

KARL BARTH

WITH A NEW INTRODUCTION BY
David Haddorff

Wipf & Stock
PUBLISHERS
Eugene, Oregon

The essay *Gospel and Law* was originally published in German by Chr. Kaiser Verlag under the title *Evangelium und Gesetz.*

Wipf and Stock Publishers
199 W 8th Ave, Suite 3
Eugene, OR 97401

Community, State and Church
Three Essays by Karl Barth With An Introduction byDavid Haddorff
By Barth, Karl
Copyright©1960 Theologischer Verlag Zurich
ISBN: 1-59244-923-9
Publication date 10/5/2004
Previously published by Anchor Books, 1960

CONTENTS

Introduction by David Haddorff—Karl Barth's Theological Politics   1

Gospel and Law   71

Church and State   101

    INTRODUCTION

    THE CHURCH AND THE STATE AS THEY CONFRONT
       ONE ANOTHER

    THE ESSENCE OF THE STATE

    THE SIGNIFICANCE OF THE STATE FOR THE
       CHURCH

    THE SERVICE WHICH THE CHURCH OWES TO THE
       STATE

The Christian Community and the Civil Community   149

Bibliography   191

Karl Barth's Theological Politics

David Haddorff
St. John's University

Writing an essay on Barth's political thought presents the particular challenge of relating his politics to his theology as a whole. The crucial point is that one must generally begin with Barth's theology before one ventures into a specific area of his thought, like politics. Failure to do this leads to both theological and political misrepresentations. The most common misreading is that Barth's Christocentric theology (and rejection of natural theology) leads to an ambivalent and even bewildering view of theological politics. Such is the view of Will Herberg's extensive essay, "The Social Philosophy of Karl Barth," which was the original introduction to the 1960 printing of this book.[1] Known best for his work in sociology of religion, Herberg appreciatively traces the development of Barth's political thought from *Der Römerbrief*, whose 'transcendent word' breaks asunder all liberal utopian thought, to his defiance against Hitler's regime and the formation of the Confessing church and the writing of the Barmen Declaration. Herberg rightly argues that it was Barth's Christological conception of the state (and subsequent rejection of traditional Catholic and Protestant views of the state) that provided the substance of his theological critique of the Nazification of the state and church. Yet, for Herberg, Barth's heroic stature during the German church struggle eviscerates after World War II against Soviet communism, when a different Barth emerges. The problem is, as Herberg sees is, that Barth uses his Christocentric view to reject the anti-communism of the 1950s, and instead drift toward a middle position 'between East and West', condemning German remilitarization and nuclear proliferation. In short,

1

Barth's theological politics—because it depends on Christology—remains ambiguous and confusing; Barth's political ethics is relevant in the 1930s but not in the 1950s. It is Herberg's essay that prompts John Howard Yoder to say that Barth's political thought is a "continuing story rather than . . . an oscillation between 'now you have an ethic' and 'now you don't,' an oscillation for which one cannot find a respectful explanation."[2] Yoder's core argument against Herberg is that he misunderstands the later Barth because he misunderstands his theology as a whole, and its relation to the ongoing Evangelical tradition in theology. Yoder, in the 1960s–70s, was one of the first to adequately describe the internal consistency of Barth's theological ethics, and its how it led to a particular yet open-ended political trajectory.

Since Herberg's essay there has been renewed interest in the political Barth. In addition to Yoder, a fresh view of the political Barth emerged in Europe, especially through the work of Frederich-Wilhelm Marquardt, who argued that Barth never really broke with socialism, but provided a new Christological foundation for socialism in the *Church Dogmatics*.[3] Although generally rejected today, Marquardt's thesis rightly presents Barth not as a non-political dogmatician, but as a theologian who politically engaged his own social-historical circumstances. More recently, in *Against Hegemony*, Timothy Gorringe continues this line of thinking, demonstrating how Barth's dogmatics must be interpreted in response to the various hegemonies he confronted, including theological liberalism, Religious Socialism, Nazism, political nationalism, *lassiez-faire* capitalism, and both communism and anti-communism.[4] Barth offers more than a No to hegemony, says Gorringe; he also offers the Yes of freedom and liberation grounded in the Word of God. Gorringe's political reading of Barth as a kind of proto-liberation theologian remains one perspective, among many, that have emerged in the last decade exploring his theological ethics, including his political thought.[5] Perhaps the most important book on Barth's politics is Frank Jehle's *Against the Steam*, which clearly presents a political Barth actively engaging politics throughout his life.[6]

The overall consensus is that he was political, and his thought remains important to this day.

The way Barth addressed political issues always begins with his theological presumptions. In agreement with Alan Torrance, Barth's thought is better seen as a kind of "theological politics" rather than the more popular term, "political theology."[7] Unlike many approaches of political theology that tend to speak about theology within a political framework (theology interpreted *politically*), Barth reverses this view and speaks about politics within a theological framework and its relationship to the church (politics interpreted *theologically*).[8] Unlike Barth's approach, political theology usually begins with a social-scientific analysis of the state and civil society (including the church), and then correlates theological belief or practice. Theology becomes an appendage to language of political science, sociology, or political philosophy. In contrast, Barth develops a political perspective based entirely upon God's action in and through the revelation of the Word of God. His commitment to the Word of God led him to be a dialectical thinker moving between absolute Yes and No, between absolute positive or negative views of the state, between absolute Christian claims of the legitimacy of the state and anarchic denial of legitimacy, between Marxist socialism and free market capitalism, and between right-wing nationalism and left-wing revolutionary politics. Once these extreme ideologies are ruled out, Barth remains committed to a practical "*non-ideological politics, strictly orientated toward political issues themselves.*"[9] His practical politics led him to be generally supportive—but not an apologist—for liberal constitutional democracy and a more left-leaning 'social market' position of economic justice. And although he presumed that the state was to be the *guardian* of the common good, which meant using force to protect the state, he also saw the state called to a higher purpose of peace and justice, namely to be a *witness* to the kingdom of God.

This essay looks more at the issue of how the church and state (and world) relate to one another and less at the issue of war. Nevertheless, it is my contention that Barth moved between the absolutes of just war and absolute pacifism and

3

promoted an active peacemaking role for the state.[10] Barth's peacemaking perspective (or as he called it, "practical pacifism") is not a reversal of an earlier just war position, but remained his continuing perspective, like his commitment to democratic socialism, throughout his life. Once war begins, however, the state (and Christians within it) must choose between participating and not participating, between supporting the state's decision and not supporting that decision.[11] For example, Barth's general commitment to the state led him to say No to violence in 1914, but Yes in 1939; by the 1950s, in a time of relative peace, he returned to a more definitive No position. This is not a reversal of positions, but movement within a dialectical position that begins with the peacemaking function of the state, but also acknowledges that there are very unusual circumstances when the state can only preserve peace through the use of force. Barth's understanding of Christian witness allows the Christian to move freely between an affirmative Yes or No, in response to what God's commands require in particular circumstances. To forget that Barth's ethics is one of openness and movement is to forget his basic point, namely that ethics is responsible action in *relation* to God's command of grace.

Therefore, this essay presents a continuous—yet dialectical—portrait of Barth's theological politics, which includes the following points: 1) like all theology, his theological politics is not an independent science but one that begins with the revelation of the Word of God and the deliberative response of the Christian community (church); 2) politics begins with God's action in Jesus Christ, in judgment and grace, which negatively delegitimizes all ideologies, but also positively commands responsible (and non-ideological) political action; 3) like theology, political thought is dialectical, namely, it remains in constant movement of distinguishing and relating without falling into the extremes of separation and identification; and 4) this dialectical movement allows him to move back and forth, taking different positions at different times, while remaining firmly committed to the priority of God's action in history; and 5) by placing both church and state within the kingdom of God, he rejects the

4

extreme positions of, on one side, the church standing absolutely *against* the 'demonic' state, and, on the other, the church standing absolutely *for* the 'divine' state, and instead affirms the church standing *with* the secular—yet redeemed—state.

Finally, we must remember that Barth *lived* this theology as well as wrote about it; we cannot separate the man from his thought. Hence, it is important to examine the historical context of the three essays included in this volume, in light of Barth's life and the development of his theology as a whole. With this in mind, this essay includes four parts: 1) a brief political biography of Barth; 2) important themes prior to the publication of "Gospel and Law" (1935); 3) a description of the three essays, "Gospel and Law," Church and State", and the "Christian Community and the Civil Community"; and 4) Barth's later thought and his relevance for contemporary discussions in theological politics.

The Political Barth

Barth's first political involvement was as a theology student in 1904, when he joined the Swiss Zofinger Union of Bern, the oldest student political union in Switzerland, dating back to 1819.[12] This liberal union supported constitutional republican governmental reform, including the rights of public assembly, trial by jury, freedoms of speech and press, and the right of self-government. No doubt as a student he became further interested in Religious Socialism, which was making a significant impact in Switzerland during the first decade of the twentieth century through the efforts of Leonhard Ragaz (1868–1945), Hermann Kutter (1963–1931), and the German Christoph Blumhardt (1858–1919). When Barth was called to his first pastorate at Safenwil in 1911, he not only served the spiritual needs of the congregation, but as a theological liberal and a committed Religious Socialist, he sought to address their economic ones as well.[13]   Later, in 1915, the 'Red pastor at Safenwil' decided to join the Social Democratic party, not out of ideological commitment, but to stand in *solidarity* with the working-class members of his congregation who joined the party, and suffered various injustices in their factory work. In addition to his ministerial duties, he helped form local unions, began serving as a party delegate, and attended socialist conferences.

Barth's activity in politics was matched, if not superseded, by his serious commitment to the relevance of theology. He longed for an authentic voice for theology in the world; this, in fact, is why he turned to Religious Socialism in the first place. Regardless, the young Reformed pastor's life was first tested in 1914, when neither the liberal establishment of German theology nor Religious Socialism were able to challenge the political war aims of Kaiser Willhem II. It was the disruption of World War I, and its horrendous aftermath, that forced Barth to question the liberal theology that undermined the church's commitment to the nationalistic and militaristic goals of Germany and the other nations.[14] Barth struggled to develop a theology that began with the otherness of God and challenged the political, moral, and religious, idealistic aims of humanity, which had collapsed in the War.[15] This turn toward theological objectivism, and critical realism, begins with the premise that to take human moral action seriously, we must first take *God* seriously; the problem, however, is that liberal theology, and consequently Religious Socialism, had turned this basic principle around.[16] God's otherness reveals a *diastasis* that exists between human righteous actions, including political praxis, and God's righteous action. Therefore, if he was to begin in a different place than the anthropocentrism and immanentism of liberal theology (and much Religious Socialism), then he would have to take God seriously and open himself to the otherness of God's mystery and revelation.

Barth's theological struggle was essentially with the liberal theology behind Religious Socialism and not with overall commitment to social justice and its practical policies. We may recall that the two most important Swiss socialists who had direct influence on Barth were Leonhard Ragaz and Herman Kutter. Ragaz, more of a classic left-wing activist, merged his Christian beliefs into the secular movement of Social

6

Democracy, and sought to work with other secular socialists in seeking the goals of pacifism and social justice. In contrast, Kutter, who was less political and more prophetic, envisioned the kingdom of God emerging only with God's action. Kutter believed that God would use both religious and secular movements, like Marxism, to bring about these socialist changes. On the surface, Barth *politically* supported Ragaz's practical commitments to change the political and economic structures of injustice and his stance against political nationalism and the war. It would seem odd to preach and teach Christian socialism, but not actually attempt to transform the human structures that would necessarily lead to these changes. On a deeper level, however, Barth became more *theologically* sympathetic to Kutter's "watching and waiting" perspective, which shifted the focus from human action to divine action, thus more generally, from humanity to God. Although he disagreed with Kutter's politics, he became convinced that if the socialist movement would lead to God's kingdom, it would have to be God's doing, not humanity's.[17] Leaning toward Kutter, therefore, in 1915, Barth met the German Lutheran Pietist Christoph Blumhardt, who had significant influence on both Ragaz and Kutter. Blumhardt had previously been active in Social Democratic politics and even served in the German parliament a decade earlier. The theology of Christoph and his father Johann Christoph Blumardt (1805–80) appealed to Barth because it offered a strictly eschatological and God-centered understanding of God's action in this world in its total human context, in terms of both the personal and social good. The younger Blumhardt's theology involved waiting upon God's action but also hastening toward full realization of the eschatological hope; the kingdom of God is both present and future, and remains entirely dependent upon God's action through 'Jesus the Victor.' Unlike the more extreme positions of Ragaz and Kutter, Blumhardt offered a dialectical position, which Barth found appealing, and provided a good argument against the ideological theory of Religious Socialism.[18]

The most acute and salient theme during Barth's World War I writings is the obvious reminder that God *is* God and we are not! By 1916 he wrote essays on God's righteousness and the "Strange World of the Bible," both of which reveal a significant *diastasis* between God and humanity, between the world of the Bible and our world.[19] If we are to be true to 'God's otherness' as revealed in the strangeness of the Bible, we must go beyond allowing it to provide *answers*—as was the case in liberal theology and Religious Socialism—and allow it to provide the *questions* we seek to ask. These early writings culminate in his 1918 commentary on the *Epistle to the Romans (Der Römerbrief)*, where he further challenges liberal anthropocentrism, Pietism, Religious Socialism, Idealistic ethics, and established religion (including Christianity, or preferably Christendom).[20] Although he continued to support the Swiss social democratic movement, he denounced the self-divinization of Religious Socialism, and its apparent blending of divine and human action in and through the socialist movement. Christians were to remain committed to social democracy but not 'Religious Socialism.' In the revolutionary year of 1918, Barth called Christians to remain committed to the otherness and radicalness of God's kingdom, which cannot be ushered in through human action, nor verbalized and actualized in any human ideology. If there is a legitimate form of politics, it must be theological *and* non-ideological.

These themes continue in Barth's 1919 'Tambach lecture,' which served as a bridge between the theology of the first and second editions of *Der Römerbrief*. This speech redirected his Religious Socialist audience away from a strict identification of their action with God's divine action, and toward Christ, who is and remains the source of both the Christian's "affirmation" and "criticism," both the Yes and No, of the social order.[21] Since Barth views moral action as an analogy or parable of divine action, the Christian view of society should neither be entirely culture-affirming nor culture-denying, but a mixture of both and seen in light of God's Yes and No. Nevertheless, by this time Religious Socialism in Switzerland was in disarray. In 1919 it had split into two groups, with the more radical wing joining the 'Third Communist International' and forming the Swiss Communist party, and the more moderate wing continuing to support

8

earlier platforms of the Social Democratic party. Belonging to this latter group, Barth rejected Bolshevism as well as the moderate-capitalism of the Weimar republic in Germany. Both movements failed to take true democratic socialism seriously, so neither provided any future example for Swiss politics. So, although Barth denounced the *theory* of Religious Socialism, he continued to remain active in *practical* politics. God's No against ideology provides an opening for the Yes of political action! This subtle shift toward the Yes of political responsibility is evident in *Romans, 2ⁿᵈ edition,* published in 1922. Barth continues his attack on ideologies that underlie power politics, whether left or right. Unlike *Romans 1,* however, which was more critical of the principle of legitimation linked with the conservative/nationalist establishment, the second edition, written in the aftermath of the Bolshevik Revolution, is more critical of the principle of revolution liked with the idealistic hope for a new regime. This disparagement is counterbalanced by a more extensive discussion of Christian ethics grounded in love, which provides the basis for a more positive political ethic. Barth sees the love ethic as a "parable" or analogy of God's actions of love, which can lead to "an unconditional, genuine preference for the good of the other."[22]

Barth left Safenwil and was appointed Professor of Reformed Dogmatics at Göttingen in 1921, where he immersed himself in the historical tradition of theology and proclaimed its importance for the contemporary church. In this way, Barth began seeing himself as standing *within* the church rather than as a critic or prophet on the margins of the church, or worse yet outside the church. Although he continued to support democratic socialism throughout the 1920s, his journey into dogmatics sealed his fate with the Religious Socialists. By turning to dogmatics as the way to speak about ethics, he continued to demonstrate his desire for a theological politics rather than a political theology. Barth began seeing that theology offers a distinctive viewpoint for ethics and politics, which cannot be found in philosophy or the sciences. This is not a radical departure from his earlier period, but in fact the logical outcome of his *Romans* period; it was an attempt to provide a theology that can bear witness to God's revealed truth. Barth's dogmatic theology was further refined while serving as professor at Münster in 1925 and at Bonn in 1930. It was during this time that he gave his *Ethics* lectures.[23] These lectures set in motion the basic themes that would occupy him throughout his career, including the revelation of the Word of God, its threefold embodiment in God's actions of creation, reconciliation, and redemption, and the divine command that emerges within these relational spheres. In these lectures, we see a *culmination* of his early thought, where the No of God's judgment is matched by the Yes of God's commanding Word; where the vertical diastasis is matched by horizontal responsibility for the good of the other. Despite the fact that God's Word stands in judgment of all human ethical speech, it also provides the opportunity to encounter the good, through the divine command, which draws us toward *hearing* and then *responding* to God's Word. Barth's No to ideology, whether left or right, is also supplemented by the Yes of responsible action within civil society and the state. He endorses neither revolution nor the political status quo, but calls for a democratic movement for a more peaceful and just society. In themes that go back to the *Romans* period, Barth develops a view of society, culture, and the state in which they are neither demonic nor divine, but are affirmed through the relationship of humanity (and the world) and the Word of God, revealed in creation, reconciliation, and redemption.

Beginning in the tumultuous years of the early 1930s, Barth's life seems to accelerate in constant movement. He was not only conducting his normal duties of teaching and writing, but actively organizing and consolidating the Christian response to the emerging church conflict over the rise of Adolph Hitler and National Socialism in Germany. Remaining somewhat practically aloof from German politics during the Weimar era, in 1931 the Swiss professor joined the German Social Democratic Party—like he did the Swiss party years before—because he believed this was the most hopeful and *practical* means by which society could maintain a healthy political system. Barth's worst fears were realized when Hitler rose to power in 1933 and began dismantling the Weimar Republic and religious freedom in Germany. The nationalist ideology of the German Christian movement began to spread into the Lutheran and Reformed (Evangelical) churches. In the spring of 1933, a constitution was created that established a united German Evangelical Church, with a strong hierarchical polity including the new office of 'Reich bishop.' This shift in ecclesiastical polity proved to be not only a victory of the Lutheran church over less numerous Reformed, but a *specific* branch of Lutheranism, including the German Christians, that desired to strengthen the office of bishop within the church and develop a closer relationship to the state. The German Christian movement was the offspring of liberal theology and German nationalism; theologically they were anthropocentric and immanentist and ideologically they supported the National Socialist party, including its rejection of Marxism, Jewish German nationality, internationalism, interracial degeneration. When Hitler became Chancellor in January 1933, the German Christians were already well organized into a substantial movement and thus would have considerable influence on the Evangelical church. Yet after the constitution of the new national church was written in the spring of 1933, to the dismay of the German Christians, their principle candidate for the office, Ludwig Muller, was not elected. Nevertheless, Hitler's government in July had taken significant action by meddling in church affairs with the replacement of church and state administrators, seeking to control local synods and consistories, which led to a rewriting of the constitution and the elevation of Muller into the office of Reich bishop in 1934.

In response to these events, Martin Niemoller, a friend of Barth's, formed the Pastor's Emergency League in 1933, which later became the basis for the Confessing church. Although largely conservative and patriotic (many supported Hitler's regime), this group of pastors and some academics stood against the emerging Nazification of the church. Their main concern was the state's infringement upon the church. Barth's uncompromising *No* to Hitler and the German Christians made him a target for both admiration and disparagement.[24] He became the principal theological voice of

11

the Confessing church movement principally through his contacts and the publication of a new pamphlet series, *Theologishe Existenz heute*, which was first published in 1933, and the drafting of the Barmen Declaration (1934), which remained this movement's primary confessional document. Barth's theological attack against the heretical German Christians was based on their liberal theological underpinnings (i.e., natural theology), the false understanding of the church based on race and nationality, and their gospel which emerged from a particular political ideology. In the Barmen Declaration, with Barth as its principal author, the Confessing church made a public commitment and confession to the exclusiveness of Jesus Christ as Lord of the church and state. At its core, Barmen was a theological document, but it did have political implications for the church and state. It was against the takeover of the church by the German Christians and their strict coordination of church and state, of gospel and politics, which corrupted the church internally through heretical dogma and externally by absolutizing the power of the state. No doubt Barth was personally critical of the Nazi's anti-Semitism, and later regretted that the document did not take a firmer stand against this horrid ideology, yet he needed to compromise with those who criticized the 'Aryan paragraph' in its application *only* to the church but not the state. Although he continued to give speeches, his works were banned, and when he refused, as a professor, to give public allegiance to Hitler's rule, Barth was expelled from Germany in July, 1935.

Shortly after his return to Switzerland, Barth became a professor at the University of Basel. Although through the latter 1930s he principally worked on *Church Dogmatics*, he did publish the two essays of political importance, namely "Gospel and Law" and "Church and State", which are included in this volume. Once the war began, in his political speeches and writings, he became increasingly critical of Swiss neutrality, and how Swiss collaboration with Germany restricted certain freedoms and liberties within Switzerland. In fact, by 1941 the Swiss government censured his speeches, and eventually banned him from giving public speeches altogether, and even tapped his phones. In Barth's mind, it was more responsible to be true to the convictions of justice and freedom, and allow refugees a place to live, and accept the possibility of hardship and war than to lose your freedom and dignity as a nation, and gain peace, employment, and food. Barth's critical stance against the Swiss government led to ongoing tense relationship between Barth and state authorities throughout the post-war years, and even until his death in 1968.

After the end of the war, Barth changed his political message from one of resistance to the Nazi regime to one of forgiveness and reconciliation with Germany; thus, political responsibility had shifted from resistance against evil to helping a neighbor in need. It was in 1946 that Barth wrote arguably his most important essay in theological politics, also included in this volume, entitled "The Christian Community and the Civil Community." This essay builds upon earlier themes in Barmen and "Church and State," but draws a stronger more intimate analogical connection between church and state within their relationship to Christ's kingdom. In contrast to his early writings where a negative tension between church and state predominates, in this essay a positive relation between the two predominates. He remains faithful to his non-ideological understanding of politics, but not unlike his *Ethics* lectures, genuinely prefers a constitutional liberal democratic state to other forms, whether of the far right or left. This commitment is obvious in a series of short political writings collected in *Against the Stream.*[25] Since there is no "perfect system" of government (just "better or worse ones"), says Barth, a "proper state will be one in which the concepts of order, freedom, community, power, and responsibility are balanced in equal proportions, where none of these elements is made an absolute dominating all the others" (95). Far from idealizing one viewpoint, however, Barth adds that Christians may "speak very conservatively today and very progressively or even revolutionarily tomorrow—or vice versa"(91). "Christian politics are always bound to seem strange," and, he adds, "incalculable and surprising in the eyes of the world—otherwise they would not be Christian" (92). It was

13

the 'strangeness' of Barth's stand 'between West and East,' between a Christian 'anti-communism' and a Christian 'pro-communism,' that led to a growing controversy over his political views. He was severely criticized for not taking a negative stance against Soviet aggression, like he had done against Nazi Germany. For the Swiss theologian there was a difference. In 1949 he wrote: "Ten years ago we said that the Church is, and remains, the Church, and must not therefore keep an un-Christian silence. Today we say that the Church is, and remains, the Church, and must not therefore speak an un-Christian word" (137). Barth's controversial 'silence' concerning Soviet communism was rooted in a practical (not ideological) politics that was governed by what was most *practically* beneficial to persons within their communities. In the emerging world of the Cold War and the threat of nuclear weapons, Barth's position 'between West and East' became the logical outgrowth to his commitment to an ideologically free politics that strove for peace and justice. For Barth the main difference between the Nazis and the Soviet Communists was that the latter was blatantly atheist and secular and did not attempt to cloak itself in the form of nationalist Christianity, as did the former. It was the integrity of the church and its gospel that was primarily at stake. Moreover, because the state is neither divine nor demonic it is not necessary, at every instance, to blatantly eulogize or condemn every historical manifestation of the state; sometimes the church must simply be silent and wait, while continuing to bear witness to Christ's rule. Barth saw it as unnecessary to jump on the anti-communist bandwagon because he had doubts that this inflammatory rhetoric would really succeed in the long run, and, indeed, may eventually lead to violent conflict, possibly even nuclear war. Today, after the fall of the Soviet empire, his stance seems to be a rather moot point; he appears more of a long-sighted prophet than a short-sighted anti-patriot, which he was seen as at the time.

Meanwhile, during the 1950s and 60s, he was pressing his Christian humanist concern that the church—and the state—as the 'inner and outer circles' of the kingdom stand in solidarity with *all* humanity. Barth's Christian humanism led him to

14

defend human rights and the peacemaking function of the state. As Stalinist atrocities became better known, he often publicly denounced the tyranny of Stalin, as he had Hitler. In *The Christian Life*, for example, he argued that the "lordless power" of "leviathan" was exemplified in twentieth-century Fascism, National Socialism, *and* Stalinism.[26] Moreover, in 1958, Barth, as a participant in the *Kirchliche Brudershaften* (church brotherhoods), took further action through the writing of a petition (*Anfrage*) addressed to the Synod of the Evangelical Church in Germany. This document remained critical of West Germany's rearmament (as a member of NATO) and, more importantly, the continuing proliferation of nuclear weapons. "The prospect of a future war to be waged with the use of modern means of annihilation has created a new situation, in the face of which the Church *cannot* remain *neutral*." [27] Barth's stance against the preparation, development, and deployment of nuclear weapons remained perhaps his last great cause; a cause in which the church could rightly declare a *status confessionis*.

In summary, Barth's political thought was theologically critical and dialectical. It was critical in that he discriminated among positions and unmasked the hidden ideological commitments that stand contrary to the Word of God, and dialectical in that he often maneuvered between two uncompromising poles of thought, that is, between an absolute Yes and No. Yet in this movement, there was a lifelong persuasion toward a socialist-democratic conception of constitutional liberal democracy. In *Against the Stream*, he writes: "[A] proper State will be one in which the concepts of order, freedom, community, power and responsibility are balanced in equal proportions, where none of these elements is made an absolute dominating all the others" (96). Barth's concern, above all, was with human freedom and responsibility before God. Toward the end of his life, Barth said his concern with human freedom and responsibility, as a basic "style" and "human posture," could be characterized as a "liberal" attitude, and could be applied both to his theology and politics. He said,

15

when I call myself liberal what I primarily understand by the term is an attitude of responsibility. For freedom is always a responsible thing. And that means further that I have always to be open—here we come, do we not, to what is usually meant by freedom. Being truly liberal means thinking and speaking in responsibility and openness on all sides, backwards and forwards, toward both the past and in the future, and what I call a total personal modesty. To be modest is not be skeptical; it is to see what one thinks and says also has limits. This does not hinder me from saying very definitely what I think I see and know. But I can do this only with the awareness that there have been and are other people before and along-side me, and that others still will come after me. This awareness gives me inner peace, so that I do not think I always have to be right even though I do say definitely what I say and think. Knowing that a limit is set for me too, I can move cheerfully within it as a free man. [28]

From Safenwil to Barmen:
Early Themes in Barth's Thought

In this section we examine more closely several early writings, from *Der Römerbrief* to the Barmen Declaration (1918–34), with the purpose of developing the main *themes* of Barth's theology of politics. All these writings were written before the essays included in this volume, yet prove to be benchmarks for these later essays and his later political writings. The themes explored are: 1) his *dialectical* reasoning; 2) how this shapes his view of secular society's relationship to the church; 3) how this leads to his No against political ideology but Yes for political responsibility; 4) how it further affects his view of church and state in the Barmen Declaration; and 5) his criticism of natural theology.

Since all later themes are dependent upon the first, we begin with the dialectical pattern of Barth's theology. In

16

contrast to the earlier scholarship of Hans Urs von Balthasar, which insisted on a radical shift in Barth's thinking from his dialectical stage of the 1920s to 'analogical' stage of the 1930s and beyond, today there is a general consensus, following Bruce McCormack, that both dialectical and analogical themes existed throughout his work.[29] There is, in short, both *diastasis* and *synthesis* in the *Church Dogmatics* and also his earlier works, including his lectures on the 'Reformed Confessions', 'John Calvin', 'Ethics', and 'Dogmatic theology', all given while in Germany prior to 1931, and now published in English.[30] These works show a continuity of thought between the Romans period and the *Church Dogmatics* a decade later. The link between these two periods of Barth's thought is grounded in Barth's newly developed Christology in the mid-1920s, which enabled him to speak about the eternal Word as both veiled and unveiled, both hidden and revealed, in the humanity of Jesus Christ.[31] There is no doubt Barth's theology changed over time, but it does not consist of radical disruptions in method or thought as was previously supposed. In fact, it is the combination of being theologically open-ended, while remaining centered on the Word of God, which remains the core of his dialectical method.

So what is meant by *dialectical*? We may distinguish between two kinds of dialectical thinking, with one being vertical and the other horizontal; one being the relationship of human and divine and the other relating to human thought more generally. For Barth, the horizontal dialectic depends entirely upon the vertical. Both kinds are developed in his 1922 lecture, "The Word of God and the Task of Ministry." Here Barth argues that the task of theology remains a difficult but a necessary task of the church. Because of their sinfulness, theologians, like all persons, can only speak about God with caution and embarrassment, yet because God has spoken through God's Word, theologians must give an account of this revelation. "We must recognize both, our obligation and our inability, and thereby give God the glory."[32]   Like Calvin, Barth argues there is distance, a *diastasis*, between God and humanity that cannot be bridged by human reason, but by God's revelation, which, through grace, is accommodated to

17

sinful human reason.[33] This implies that the task of theology, and human thought more generally, must also remain cautious about its ability to make absolute statements of Yes or No, grounded in foundationalist reasoning. Dialectical thinking, says Barth, must "correlate every position and negation one against the other, to clarify 'Yes' by 'no' and 'No" by 'yes' with persisting longer than a movement in a rigid Yes or No."[34] So, unlike Hegel's dialectical method, where what is posited and negated is unified in a higher synthesis, Barth's use of dialectical reasoning emerges first from the vertical *diastasis* between God and humanity, but extends to the horizontal *diastasis* of human reasoning. As McCormack put it: "Barth's dogmatic method presupposes an initial dialectical movement of negation in which God's judgement is invite to fall on all previous efforts (including our own)." [35]Still, because God has spoken to us in Jesus Christ, the synthesis of the divine and human, the 'No' of human sin is also addressed by God's Yes of reconciliation. This makes the task of theology and political ethics (as well as other sciences) possible but not infallible. In his early thought the vertical diastasis of judgment prevails, which provides difficulties for Barth to explain the task of Christian ethics. As his theology becomes more Christological, more centered on the Word of God, he begins to develop a stronger theological basis for ethics and political responsibility. These themes are more fully developed in essays after the later 1930s, including the essays found in this volume, later political writings, and the *Church Dogmatics*. Even in these writings, however, the negative judgment remains. Jesus Christ, the Word of God, makes human knowledge possible but also always stands in judgment of such knowledge.

Second, it was Barth's Christologically centered dialectical thought in the 1920s that enabled him to move beyond his earlier *diastasis* of Christ and culture (crisis), and instead offer a new dialectical construal, of both crisis and hope, grounded in the divine-human nature of Jesus Christ.[36] In his 1926 essay "Church and Culture," Barth rejects Schleiermacher's, and liberal theology's, optimistic theology of culture emerging from its union with God's Spirit through religious consciousness, and instead argues that the "work of culture takes its place among the earthly signs by which the Church must make God's goodness, his friendship for men, visible to itself and the world."[37] In short, culture needs to be dedivinized before it can be sacralized or humanized. His dialectical theology stands both against and for culture, principally because the Word is *with* culture in the humanity of Jesus Christ. [38] Moreover, this leads to a similar dialectical understanding of how non-theological sources ought to be used in theological ethics. In contrast to the method of modern theology that begins with human experience and reason and then correlates the inner world of faith to that objective world, Barth begins with the objective world of faith and then integrates the outer world of human experience and reason. Yet Christians have a duty to seriously listen to the voices of others. Just as the Word mysteriously comes to the person its otherness, so too, she must be attentive to the Word in the *other*. Christians must remain skeptical, however, of other *words* replacing or altering the message of the Word of God. This was the correlationalist strategy of "apologetics" that he rejected in his early writings, which he equates with liberal theology and Schleiermacher. [39] This is when theology relies on the use of any correlative or synthetic principle, as articulated by the conjunction *and*, which places on equal footing theology with other non-theological sources. If there is to be a theology of politics, it must begin with the Word of God, but cannot presume that God may speak in the voice of the other, including non-theological sources.

The third theme explores how Barth's dialectical thought serves as the basis for Barth's *critical* stance toward political ideology but also an *affirmation* for political responsibility. We begin first with his No against ideology. It was pointed out that Barth's early search for the otherness of God finds its fruition in *Romans I*.[40] In his discussion of Romans 13:1-7, Barth distances himself both from traditional Protestant legitimating of political authority, whether the Lutheran 'two kingdoms' or the Reformed 'orders of creation' theology, and instead seeks to *contrast* the state with God's kingdom. Against the various ideologies that caused and supported the

19

Great War in mind, Barth's No is louder than his Yes; he emphatically rejects the hegemony and legitimacy of the state and political ideology that underlies power politics.[41] The Christian task remains neither to maintain or transform the state but to "replace it" with the kingdom of God, which can only be ushered in by "God's revolution" (504). True revolutionary politics seeks to replace the human state with God's state; Christians are to "starve the state religiously" (508). Does this imply that Barth is an anarchist? What does it mean, in Pauline language, to "be subject to governing authorities"? Barth responds that although "God's revolution" is God's action, Christians can prepare for it by acting in solidarity with others and critically engaging the existing society and its institutions. Barth rejects anarchism because he argues that Christians do have political obligations such as paying taxes, engaging in political activity, and military service, yet they are to accept political authority and fulfill their political duties "without illusions." God uses the state to protect the innocent from injustice and to punish evildoers. Yet, since the state belongs to the 'old aeon', Christian duties to the state should never be seen as intrinsically "Christian duties"; Christians must never combine "throne and alter," nor should they preach "Christians patriotism" (520). Even though his sympathies lie more with the political left and revolutionary politics than with the political right and conservative reactionary politics, Barth's core argument is a politics that is *free* from all ideology.

Barth's ideological critique, as mentioned earlier, continues in his Tambach lecture and *Der Römerbrief* (2nd edition). In Tambach, he argues that Christian responsibility begins not with some abstract conception of the good, understood as an Enlightenment universal standpoint of "perfect criticism," or in the absoluteness of Christian social activism, as is the case in Religious Socialism.[42] Christians should neither simply accept the current social order or the status quo ("perfect naiveté"), nor accepting the false belief that God's kingdom is realizable through ethical action ("perfect criticism") or revolutionary protest (320). Resistance against the powers, including political power, rejects the

20

options of complacency, utopianism, or anarchy! In *Romans II*, he more persuasively grounds his eschatology and Christology, and develops for the first time an 'ethic of witness' that depends upon responding to God's divine command in Jesus Christ.[43] God's grace as judgment stands in contrast to any scheme or theory of modern anthropocentric ethics, or in Barth's more expressive language: "Grace is the axe laid at the root of the good conscience."[44] This leads Barth to be critical of both the conservative politics but also the "Titianism" of revolutionary politics, both of the political right and left.[45]

Therefore, the No of judgment is answered dialectically with the Yes of God's movement of grace, which leads to positive ethics of political responsibility. In Tambach, he admonishes his Religious Socialist audience to not abandon the world to itself, where it is "ruled by its own logos" and "its own hypostases and powers"(280). Instead, Christian action must be guided by "an *affirmation* of the world as it is" (298). "Only out of such an affirmation can come that genuine, radical denial which is manifestly the meaning of our movements of protest" (299). Human action remains only *parabolic* of divine action, and in no way is divine action, but it is still parabolic of its "heavenly analogue." Likewise, in *Romans II*, Barth distinguishes between "primary" and "secondary" ethical action, with the first being a response to God in worship, and the second a response toward our neighbor and community.[46] It is worship and prayer as "primary" ethical activities that provide the basis for other human "secondary" actions.[47] Positively speaking, "secondary" ethical action consists of love of neighbor, and, negatively speaking, any strict identification of God's command and human causes, whether political, economic, or social-cultural.

Only later in the decade, in his 1928–31 ethics lectures at Münster and Bonn, do we see the true emergence of the positive command ethics of the Word of God.[48] We are reminded that after Göttingen, Barth took positions in Münster in 1925 and Bonn in 1930 and remained in Germany until 1935, when he returned to Switzerland. Nevertheless, the

21

1920s was a significant period of development in Barth's theology, and this can be seen in his *Ethics*, which John Webster says is a "strikingly anti-modern text." "In its own way," adds Webster, "it is as subversive of some of the axioms of modernity as is the work of Heidegger and Wittgenstein."[49] Barth's theological ethics most basically is a 'Trinitarian ethics of witness' that lies "in the reality of God's commanding, of God's Word so far as it claims us men and finds our faith and obedience"(35).[50] True freedom is the freedom *for* obedience, and true obedience is freedom for the *other*, and, by implication, the various communities and institutions of society.[51] As God's "emergency orders," the church and state "both presuppose sin, and they thus embody God's order as his contracting of sin and its reality as grace and law" (243–44). Like Calvin, who saw the state as an 'external means of grace' Barth says the state

> is the sign, set up by God's revelation, of the concrete and visible order of life by which and in which, on the basis of accomplished reconciliation, we are summoned to serve our neighbor. This order, too, is effective in the free act of God's grace and, under the presupposition of this act, but *only* under it, is both a divine institution and a divine willed human society. . . It, too, is a sign of mediated fellowship between God and man. It, too, once was not and one day will not be, so that it belongs with the church to the time between the times, to the kingdom of grace. (445)

At first glance, Barth appears to be more of a social conservative in *Ethics* than in his earlier writings and in what he would write after Word War II. Yet the main trajectory of his thought remains the same, as calls for practical responsible action within the state. The church's primary task is to be a witness to the Word of God, and *remind* the state of its need for repentance and its purpose of promoting justice and peace.[52] The Christian stance is one of responsible management and *reform* of the state. Because the mission of the state is to provide for the welfare of the entire society it, and its best form, has the form of the constitutional democracy, balance of power between legislative executive and judicial powers, although in general "the power of the state comes from the people"(449). In *Ethics* we see, really for the first time, a synthesis between Barth's theological politics and practical political action within democratic society; a Christian witness to the state and the state's witness to the world. Barth's more positive theological politics is largely the success of his theological ethics as a whole. Responsible political action emerges in response to God's divine command; God's action provides the basis for human responsive action. The horizontal substance of God's command, in our relations to others, depends on its vertical substance. God brings *freedom* to the conscience and the moral life in and through our obedience and responsibility to the Word. Christian ethics is not conformity to some posited value or standard of excellence but responsible actions of "witness," says Barth, one that depends upon the *relational* action of God toward humanity. What is fundamental to the human subject is not her moral consciousness, but her relationship to God's Word.

The fourth and fifth themes explore, in more detail, the Barmen Declaration and Barth's critique of 'natural theology', which, in his view, was the underlying theological heresy of the German Christians and their apology for the Nazification of the church. Thus, it is rather shortsighted to speak about Barmen without talking about Barth's Nein to natural theology and the role that both of these play in the three essays in this volume. As stated earlier, Barth was the principal author of the 1934 Declaration of the Confessing Church at Barmen. This document includes six succinct paragraphs: 1) the church must hear and obey the one Word of God (Jesus Christ) and no other voice, person, events, powers, or sources of truth as God's revelation; 2) Jesus Christ claims our *whole* life, and rejects the idea that other "lords" rule over other areas of our lives; 3) the church, too, must not be forced to have its message altered by prevailing social ideologies or political convictions; 4) the church does have a proper form of government, but rejects the notion that there are special leaders (*Fuhrer*) of authority over and within the church; 5) draws for a separation of duties of

23

church and state, and rejects the state becoming the church and the church becoming the state; 6) the church's task and mission should not be corrupted by its pride and desire for power and prestige.

The paragraph that deals most explicitly with church and state is paragraph five, which provides glimpse into Barth's theology of church and state. It is worth quoting in full:

> "Fear God, honour the King!" (1 Pet 2:17) Scripture tells us that by divine appointment the State, in this still unredeemed world in which also the Church is situated, has the task of maintaining justice and peace, so far as human discernment and human ability makes this possible, by means of threat and use of force. The church acknowledges with gratitude and reverence towards God the benefit of this, his appointment. It draws attention to God's Kingdom (*Reich*), God's commandment and justice, and with these the responsibility of those who rule and those who are ruled. It trusts and obeys the power of the Word, by which God upholds all things. We reject the false doctrine that beyond its special commission the state should and could become the sole and total order of human life and so fulfill the vocation of the church as well. We reject the false doctrine that beyond its special commission the church should and could take on the nature, tasks and dignity which belong to the state and thus become itself an organ of the state.[53]

The content of paragraph five builds on his earlier discussion of the state in *Ethics*, but also moves beyond it in several important ways. Barth refuses to separate the state, as an 'order of preservation' (creation), from the church, as an 'order of redemption', and consequently places them into two *separate* functions and tasks. Instead, directed by divine authority, both church and state remain committed to peace and justice, in a world that is "not yet redeemed." The state is not completely governed by autonomous devilish principles of power and force, and the church by merciful spiritual principles of love

24

and hope. This false separation, in Barth's view, leads to the ideology of non-interference of the church in state affairs and the state's excessive use of force. This 'two kingdoms' theory, once grossly exaggerated, became an apologetic doctrine for the German Christians' support for the Nazi regime. Instead, Barth argued that the state is distinct (although not separate) from the church. The church, in gratitude toward God, must not seek to undermine the state's legitimate task in principle, but must draw attention or *remind* the state that God's kingdom stands above the church and state; through its *witness* to the gospel, the church reminds the state of its proper task to be a responsible agent of peace and justice in the world.

Hence, once the positive relations of church and state are explained, the document rejects a totalitarian conception of the state. When the state becomes totalitarian it takes upon itself an idolatrous spiritual function, and further challenges the church to act politically against the state. In response, the state must resist the temptation to become the sole power in society, and the church must resist the temptation to control society through the methods and strategies of the state, thus becoming an "organ of the state." It is important to remember that paragraph five does not stand on its own, but remains in concert with the other paragraphs, particularly paragraph one, which places both church and state under the "one Word of God." This Christological basis for the state becomes more saliently expressed in his later political writings, but is also present in this document as well as earlier in his *Ethics* lectures.

How was Barmen received by the opponents of the Confessing Church? The German Christians never attempted to address the theological grounding of Barmen, but only its political ramifications. As implied earlier, the German Christian movement was not strongly theological, and except for a few theologians like Emmanuel Hirsch, did not attempt to speak theologically about politics. A more important theological reaction can be noticed at an academic conference that was held at Anbasch, a few weeks after Barmen, which included many of the more well-known theologians who did not belong to the Confessing Church. This so-called Anbasch

Counsel denounced the Declaration as faulty theology because it failed to distinguish between the 'two kingdoms' and two principle loci of law and gospel, which invariably denied the existence of natural theology. Led by Lutherans like Paul Althaus and Werner Elert, the council affirmed that "God's word speaks to us as law and gospel." "The law," they added, "binds us to the natural orders to which we are subject, such as family, folk, and race (i.e., blood relationship)."[54] Indeed, regarding natural theology, Elert later wrote: "The proposition that apart from Christ no truth is to be acknowledged as God's revelation is a rejection of the divine authority of the divine law *beside* that of the gospel."[55] Since Barmen did not address the longstanding debate between Lutherans and Reformed about the relationship of the law and the gospel, what worried Elert and Althaus is that Barth was implicitly placing the gospel *before* the law, by placing them both *under* the Word of God. This pattern of *gospel-law* stands in contrast to the traditional Evangelical pattern of *law-gospel*, which on one hand affirmed the theological legitimacy of the state and orders of society, and on the other kept the gospel 'pure' by limiting its use only to the church. From this viewpoint, Barmen reflected a kind of 'anarchist theology' that undermined the authority of social institutions established in God's ordered creation. Yet, as we know, Barth was no anarchist but a democratic constitutionalist; in fact, he realized that the traditional law-gospel pattern was incapable of challenging the ideology of the German Christians, who identified the divine law with the human *laws* in society. Barth rightly surmised that this law-gospel pattern, once blended with a liberal naiveté, was the basis for the natural theology of the German Christians. A year later, in his essay "Gospel and Law," he eventually worked out his position more clearly, but before that he was forced to write his famous *Nein* to natural theology.

This debate over natural theology peaked when Barth's friend, and fellow Swiss Reformed theologian, Emil Brunner, published his pamphlet *Nature and Grace* in which he attacked Barth's apparent unbending rejection of natural theology. Brunner and Barth had been debating the theological implications for the dialectic of law and gospel for several years, and what was the proper Reformed position. On one side, Brunner insisted that the law, as a 'point of contact', prepared the way for the gospel by reveling both an incipient knowledge of sin and God's righteousness (including God's judgment), and on the other, Barth claimed that such a point of contact effectively removed the priority of the gospel, a mistake found in the 'two kingdoms' theology of the German Christians, and before that, theological liberalism. For Barth, *Nature and Grace* completely undermined the first paragraph of Barmen, namely that "Jesus Christ is the one voice" in revelation. Why Barth so vehemently responded in his essay *Nein!*, published a few months after Barmen, was the fact that Brunner's essay had won the praise of German Christian theologians like Hirsch and other mainstream confessionalists like Althaus and Elert. The fact that Brunner was Swiss Reformed and an outspoken critic of the German Christians made it more poignant, because being "closer to the truth" he was "much more dangerous." Barth has seen others like his longtime friend Fredrich Gogarten become swayed by the ideology of the German Christians, which led to the demise of their journal *Zwischen den Zeiten*, and no doubt feared that many others in the Confessing Church would be swayed by Brunner's argument in *Nature and Grace*.

Barth was sharply focused on arguments that would lead to an alternative or second source of revelation. The central error of natural theology is that it places humanity at the center of the universe, and claims to know God, apart from God's own self-revelation. To argue that God speaks in history, nature, culture, or society apart from what God has spoken in Jesus Christ is to deny the *true* revelation of the Word of God. In so doing, it denies God's freedom to act, and with it, God's own nature, or in short, it *denies God* as God is known in revelation.[56] The knowledge of God, for Barth, is always mediated through a sign or sacrament, which represents, indeed embodies, God's truth. The principal sign or sacrament of God is the humanity of Jesus Christ. When theological ethics begins with nature or creation instead of the Word made flesh, it rejects the background picture (moral ontology) that

God has revealed in history, and with it God's freedom to act. This means, for example, that when Christians formulate a political theology from the doctrine of creation or natural law, they begin at the wrong place, and endanger themselves to inevitable borrowings of non-theological viewpoints. Without the theological realism, discovered in God's revelation of the Word, a Christian form of political ethics inevitably becomes a philosophy or a theology that may be inclusive of other ideological viewpoints, but ironically not the Word. What this means is that not only theology and ethics but political thought as well can be corrupted by a reliance upon natural theology. There are only a few small steps from natural theology to the German Christians, and the German Christians to the Nazis. Barth feared that this pattern toward theological, ecclesial, and political corruption could happen anywhere, including Western Europe and the United States, where a commitment to natural theology (and liberal theology) were dominant.

Three Essays: 1935–46

In the Fall of 1935, pastor Karl Immer of Barmen asked Barth to come to that city to deliver his address *"Evangelium und Gesetz"* ("Gospel and Law") as a farewell address to Christians in Germany.[57] Once Barth began his journey, he was stopped by the Gestapo and was forced to return to Switzerland. So, in instead of Barth, Immer publicly read the address to the overflowing church at Barmen, with the Gestapo present. This important document indicates on the surface that Barth was doing theology and "only theology," yet the discussion of this document invariably had political overtones. It was a theological criticism of the German Christian falsifications of the law, and their justification for the Nazi's ideology of family, folk, and race. Still, the least known of the three essays in this volume, it is more important as a theological rationale for the later more overtly political works.

Similar to the dialectical relationship of church and state, Barth argues law and gospel can be distinguished but not separated. The false separation of ethics from theology, human

28

action from divine action, and human law from God's law, all derive from the separation of law and gospel in modern theology and ethics. This separation, says Eberhard Busch, has led to an "emancipation of ethics from the gospel of grace."[58] In other words, because the law is not 'formed' by the gospel it remains formed by other non-Christian or non-theological moral frameworks such as philosophy or the natural and social sciences; secular ethics replaces the gospel of grace with the human moral law. When ethics becomes either autonomous or heteronomous it becomes reduced to duty or strict obedience to non-theological principles. In contrast, Barth argues the divine law comes to us in "the form of the gospel," which permits persons the freedom and responsibility to act within this covenant relationship. Most basically, Christian ethics begins with God's covenantal action and not in human autonomous decision-making. This continues the same line of thinking that goes back to the *Romans* period, and forward into his *Church Dogmatics IV* (Reconciliation), concerning the relationship of human and divine agency. In the humanity of Jesus Christ, human agency is restored, healed, and allowed to live in free response to God's gracious command. Barth writes: "It is as He makes Himself responsible for man that God makes man, too, responsible."[59]

So what does it mean for the church to be responsible in its freedom? The "Church would not be the Church," says Barth, if it would not become "visible and apprehensible also for the world, for state and society," if it failed to obey the law in "its commands, its questions, its admonitions, and its accusations" (79). Indeed, he adds:

> The Church would not be the Church if these aspects of the Law would not, as such, become the prophetic witness *for* the will of God *against* all of men's sinful presumption, *against* all their lawlessness and unrighteous. Thus, we can certainly make the general and comprehensive statement that the Law is nothing else than the *necessary form of the Gospel*, whose content is grace. (79–80)

29

As the "form" and "content" of the Word of God, law and gospel are distinguished but not separated into "more and less, better and worse," or "between divine and human or good and evil!"(81). The gospel takes "priority over the law" because it declares firmly what God has done *for* us in Jesus Christ; this is the 'content' of the gospel. In contrast, the law—as form of the gospel, tells us what we must do *for* God, but only in light of the content of the gospel, of God's reconciliation of the sinner. Prayer, repentance, and forgiveness become the foundation of Christian moral action; Christian witness to the gospel leads to a free obedience of God's commands as found in the Decalogue, for example. "Thus there can never be claims and demands which would have legal validity from another source or in themselves: there can only be *witnesses*" (83). Christian witnesses are primarily concerned not with the law, but with "the grace of God, which has accomplished everything for us and whose end must be this accomplishment" (83).

Once God's law is stripped of its gracious content, its perverted form can be applied to the terms of civil law or social custom. The law cannot simply stand on its own, but has to be interpreted, or filled with a 'particular content,' which in the context of natural theology can take upon itself many social, cultural, or historical forms. In defining the gospel as the *content* of the word of God and the law as its *form*, he challenges the ideology of the German Christians. Therefore, when the German Christians argued that the gospel must be 'contextualized' or take a new 'form' in the "*Volksnomoi* (people's laws)" of nation, race, and people, this not only changes the form of the law but the content of the gospel (91). Saying this, the movements of German nationalism, civil obedience and citizenship, and even ethnic and racial purity, can all be seen as a "deformation and distortion of the Law" (91). In this case the content of the law is deformed; the Word of God is replaced with some other *word*.

In summary, the dialectic of law and gospel remains a core issue within the Reformers, and a longstanding tension between the Lutheran and Reformed traditions. By placing the gospel *before* the law, Barth reverses the usual understanding of how law and gospel interrelate. In traditional Evangelical dogmatics, the law (what God wills *from* us) in a sense prepares the heart for the gospel by declaring our sinfulness and need for God's grace, or, in short, prepares us for salvation. In contrast, the gospel (what God wills *for* us), responds to the law's preparation by releasing the repentant from sin's bondage. By placing the gospel before the law, Barth argues that "[F]rom what God does *for* us, we infer what he wants *with* us and *from* us" (78).[60]   This leads him to criticize any other law other than the one that remains the 'form' of the gospel whose 'content' is grace. He writes,

> If the Law is also *God's Word*, if it is further *grace* that God's Word is spoken aloud and become audible, and if grace means nothing else than *Jesus Christ*, then it is not only uncertain and dangerous but perverse to want to understand the Law of God on the basis of any other thing, of any other event different from the event in which the will of God, tearing in two the veil of our theories and interpretations, is visible as grace in both and content. (77)

Three years later, in 1938, Barth more resolutely shifted his theology into a more explicit political direction in *Rechtfertigung und Recht* (Justification and Justice), which later was translated with the title: "Church and State." Barth's purposes for this address were both theological and political. Most obviously, he was theologically attempting to find a positive link between God's divine action of justification and human action of justice, but politically he was advocating a notion of responsible political action that would embolden Christians in Germany, Switzerland, and Czechoslovakia against Nazi aggression.[61]   What should the human action of justice be in relation to God's prior action of justification? In the past, inadequate connections between these two led to "pietistic sterility on one hand, and the sterility of the Enlightenment on the other"(105). The pietistic error leads to a preoccupation with one's spiritual state and indifference to the

31

concerns for human justice—and often a rather pessimistic view of the state, and the enlightenment error leads to a preoccupation with human justice ("secular gospel") and indifference to God's act of justification.

Looking for the "vital" and "positive" connection between the "two realms" of Christian community and the "principalities and powers," Barth begins with the relationship of Pilate to Jesus. Even though Pilate, whose 'power comes from above', acts unjustly in condemning Jesus to death on the cross, he also was a "human created instrument" of God's act of justification. Ironically, the "Roman governor" is the "virtual founder of the Church," because had he acted correctly, according to canons of "human justice" (*Recht*), then he would have altered God's act of justification (110–11). By altering God's decision in this way the state would be in a position to "proclaim divine justification" and become a idolatrous *divine* state. So, in its "decisive movement" the state was not "true to itself" in serving human justice, yet in this failure, it placed itself under God's redemption. Pilate does in fact belong in the Creed, Barth says, but to the "second article in particular!"(114). A theological analysis of the state belongs to the "Christological sphere" (120).

Hence, both the church and state belong to Christ's kingdom. God's gracious relationship to the sinner and the church is no different than God's relationship to the "powers" of the state. All powers, even though seen by some as demonic, nonetheless, belong "originally and ultimately to Jesus Christ" (118). Barth admits that the state can deny "its true substance, dignity, function, and purpose," under God's redemption, and become idolatrous, claiming for itself its own divine myth and demanding worship (118). Yet there are "*no* circumstances in which the demonic state can finally achieve what it desires"; it is not "inevitable" that the state should become a "demonic force" and become the "Beast out of the abyss"(118–19). So, even though this demonic state may publicly stand against God's purposes in the world, the Christian cannot say No and "refuse the state his service." "A fundamental Christian No cannot be given here, because it would in fact be a fundamental No to the earthly State as such,

32

which is impossible from the Christian point of view" (142–43). The kingdom of God—not the earthly church or state—is the "true system of law, the true State" (123). Therefore, the "*heavenly* Jerusalem" can be distinguished from the "*earthly* State," but the "future kingdom" still remains a "real State" not an "imaginary" or "ideal" state (123).

Meanwhile, living 'between the times' empowers the church to give the state its *intercession*. "Far from being an *object* of worship," says Barth, "the State and it representatives need prayer *on their behalf*" (136). Christians should pray for their political authorities, pay their taxes, and obey the civil laws, not only because they *respect* their civil authority, but also to remind themselves that the church is not the sole human authority. As an agent of intercession, the church's authority resides in its "priestly duty," whether the state is just or unjust, whether it's free to preach the gospel or suffers persecution. The state deserves to be respected because it too falls under God's authority. So even though the state's power turns from "protection" to "suppression," the church will continue to grant the state power as *guardian* of the law and the common good. Nonetheless, the church must not be naïve about the power of the state. "[T]hus there is clearly no cause for the Church to act as though it lived, in relation to the State, in a night in which all cats are grey" (119). The fact remains there are 'just' and 'unjust' states, and Christians must act responsibly in each of these situations. For Christians, says Barth, the "fulfillment of political duty means rather responsible choices of authority, responsible decision about the validity of laws, responsible care for their maintenance, in a word, political action, which may also mean political struggle"(144). Being responsible to the state implies that Christians respond in moral judgment and action *to* the actions of their state without seeking to *be* the state. Indeed, this is why the church needs the state because it reminds itself that it *is* the church—not the state.

It follows that the best way for the state to serve the church is not to give it power but its *freedom*, that is, allow the church to *be* the church. The church's only task is to *be* the church, but in this role, it also "expects the best" from the state (140).

Indeed, through its work, prayer, and struggle, the church seeks to establish a "just state" (*Rechtsstadt*) that seeks to create and maintain an earthly peace and justice. What the church offers the state is what it also desires from the state, namely, "nothing but freedom" (148).

> Wherever this right [freedom] is recognized, and wherever a true Church makes the right use of it (and the free preaching of justification will see to it that things fall into their true place), there we shall find a legitimate human authority and an equally legitimate human independence; tyranny on the one hand, and anarchy on the other. Fascism and Bolshevism alike will be dethroned; and the true order of human affairs—the justice, wisdom and peace, equity and care for human welfare which are necessary to that true order—will arise. (147–48)

The freedom of the state depends upon the church *being* the church, for without this witness, the state remains clueless to its true mission. As a witness to the Kingdom, the church enlightens the state of its true calling, a "just state" (*Rechtsstadt*) whose purpose is to seek peace and justice. The demonic quality of the "unjust state," in contrast, denies the church's witness, and demands its citizens to worship or 'love' the state as they would God or to demand that its citizens believe a specific "philosophy of life" (*weltanschauung*) or ideology propagated by the state. Because of its commitment to the Word of God, the church cannot give its "unquestioning assent to the will and action of the State," since this would replace its commitment to the Word. "For the possibility of intercession for the State stands or falls within the freedom of God's Word" (139). Yet even in this case, the church can never be the *enemy* of the state by refusing to resist, when the state deviates from its task of creating and administering justice. The state is honored by the church's criticism because it helps save the state from its own misuse of power; in resisting the "unjust state" the church is being responsible to the state and God's rule over the state. "All this will be done,

34

not *against* the state, but as the church's service *for* the state! Respect for the authority of the state is indeed an annex to the priestly function of the church toward the state" (138–39). In its resistance, the church should never seek to become the state, or replace the state with a powerful church. When the church seeks to be the state, it becomes an "idolatrous church", and when the state seeks to be the church it becomes an idolatrous "clerical State" (132). The church, in its essence, is not an activist or political church; in doing so, it ceases being a *witnessing* church and replaces its task of preaching, teaching, and administering the sacraments with the temptation of political power. In bearing witness to God's justification of the sinner and the state, and acting in justice, the church remains committed to its true political task.

The third and most important essay is Barth's 1946 essay, "The Christian Community and the Civil Community." The most obvious difference from the earlier writings is that the main categories of Church (*Kirke*) and State (*Stadt*) have changed to Christian community (*Christengemeinde*) and civil community (*Bürgergemeinde*). As Yoder points out, this document stands as one of earliest testaments to how the church and state ought to interact in a post-Christendom world. [62] Instead of beginning with "institutions and offices," Barth begins with communities of persons gathered "together in corporate bodies in the service of common tasks" (150). The *Christengemeinde*, the *ecclesia*, becomes most apparent in the gathered community, of Christians "in one place, region, or country" through the Holy Spirit and who seek to hear and obey the Word of God. The *Bürgergemeinde*, in contrast, is the "commonality of all the people in one place, region, or country insofar as they belong together under a constitutional system of government that is equally valid for and binding on them all, and which is defended and maintained by force" (150). The kingdom of God remains the center of two concentric circles, of which the Christian community is the "inner circle" and the civil community is the "outer circle." Therefore, both "a simple and absolute equating" and "a simple and absolute heterogeneity" between church and state remain impossible options. Instead, "the existence of the State

35

[is] an allegory, an analogue to the Kingdom of God which the Church preaches and believes in" (169). Barth's breakthrough emerges in how these two dynamic communities remain distinct yet interdependent with each other in relation to their larger place within the Kingdom of God.

There is a differentiated hierarchy and unity of the two communities. The church is the inner circle because in hearing and obeying God's revelation it bears *witness* to the Word. The state is the outer circle because it often hears and obeys other words, most often found in social and cultural identity (natural law). It is the church's proximity to the Word that differentiates it from the state. The state is easily corrupted by selfish viewpoints and becomes "ignorant" and "pagan." "All it can do is grope around and experiment with the convictions which it derives from natural law, never certain whether it may not in the end be an illusion to rely on it as the final authority and therefore always making vigorous use, openly or secretly, of a more or less refined positivism" (164). Still, both state *and* church exist in a 'not yet redeemed' world. The church, too, becomes entrapped in its own misconceptions, ignorance, and forms of paganism. Although the state, as outer circle, is further removed from the realities of the kingdom, the church, as the inner circle, is also a political organization that often fails to perceive itself for what it really is, namely a free church committed solely to the rule of God through Jesus Christ. Both church and state are in a condition of sin *and* grace; both are corruptible institutions that are, in the eschatological sense, fully redeemed. Yet until the kingdom is fully realized, the church and state (and society) remain in invariably in tension. Although, he clearly states the church, in its witness, should be a 'nonconformist' community, and ought not to look to the world for its own identity and vision, but neither should it only look to itself *apart* from its relation to the outer circle. "The real church must be the model prototype of the real State" (186). This is not because he idealizes the church, but because *only* the church remains committed to prioritizing the Word of God over the secular ideologies, myths, and philosophies that degenerate God's name in the world, thus providing a clear witness to the purpose of the state as the outer circle of the kingdom.

Like *Rechtfertigung und Recht*, Barth argues that the state serves the church by giving it *freedom* to witness, but by proposing an allegorical or analogical relationship between these two communities, he finds more specific ways to link them together. Avoiding both the demonic and divine temptations, the "just state" (*Rechtsstadt*), even in its true secularity, seeks to safeguard "both the external, relative, and provisional freedom of the individuals and the external and relative peace of their community" (150). The constitutional democratic state, as *guardian*, is preserved through its agencies or "forms," namely "legislation" or the making of laws; the "government and administration" which applies the legislation; and the "administration of justice" which practically applies these laws to particular cases of apparent injustice (150). This threefold system, Barth admits, is most consistent with constitutional democracy and the just state. Politically speaking, he admits "that the Christian line that emerges from the Gospel betrays a striking tendency to the side of what is generally called the democratic state" (181). Nonetheless, although democracy is preferred, there is nothing sacrosanct about its governmental form, as it is possible for even a just state to incorporate any governmental political system from monarchy, aristocracy, and even dictatorship. Still, without the safeguard of a balance of power legally sanctioned within a constitution, it is much easier for these autocratic systems to become a totalitarian state (*Totalstaat*). There is nothing that presumes that a democracy will always seek order over chaos, justice over injustice, and peace over violent conflict. Yet, it is naïve to assume that all government systems are the same, and they all reflect the purposes of the "just constitutional state" (*Rechsstaat*).

Therefore, Barth repeats earlier themes when he insists that governmental systems are part of God's providential plan, in that they preserve order, peace, and justice within the human community by protecting it from various forms of social disorder, violence, and injustice. The threat of political coercion provides the justification for benevolent use of

37

political power and the establishment of civil law within a particular community. The task of the just state should seek to balance the power of individual rights and responsibilities with community rights and responsibilities. The power of the state should not be concentrated either in individualism or collectivism; Barth dialectically opposes the extremes of anarchy and individualism on one hand, and totalitarian and collectivism on the other, because they both deny the 'law' that both limits and establishes human freedom. This "two-fold law," of limiting and establishing, of "no exemption from and full protection by the law," is what makes a constitutional state *just* and legitimate and preferable to other forms of political government (172). A constitutional state grounds its authority, not in arbitrary judgments or whimsical power plays, but seeks to base its authority on principles of justice that transcend mere social convention. As a moral realist, Barth assumes that once the state seeks to ground its civil law in the moral law, it seeks to obey the command of God, even though it may not completely understand this command, as a gracious command. For this knowledge, it must seek to rely upon the *witness* of the Christian community. So even though the state is ignorant of its true center and calling, it desperately needs the church to remind it of its true purposes, functions, and goals. The church stands as a humane reminder that the task of the state is to preserve and defend human freedom, hope, and justice.

> However much human error and human tyranny may be involved in it, the State is not a product of sin but one of the constants of the divine Providence and government of the world in its action against human sin: it is there an instrument of divine grace. The civil community shares both a common origin and a common center with the Christian community. . . . Its existence is not separate from the Kingdom of Jesus Christ; its foundations and its influence are not autonomous. It is outside the Church but not outside the range of Christ's domination—it is an exponent of His kingdom. . . . [This] makes one thing quite

impossible, however: a Christian decision to be indifferent; a non-political Christianity. The Church can in no case be indifferent or neutral towards this manifestation of an order so clearly related to its own mission. Such indifference would be equivalent to the opposition of which it is said in Romans 13:2 that it is a rebellion against the ordinance of God—and rebels secure their own condemnation. (156–57)

The church stands neither absolutely *against* the state, nor does it stand always uncritically *for* the state, but its stands dialectically *with* the state. The state is genuinely secular, and for it to be otherwise would be to deny its distinction from the church. Since the church encourages the state to be the state in all its secularity, there can be no such thing as a Christian state or Christian political party. The church cannot promote a particular form of government or party to the exclusion of others, without seeking to be itself the state. In fact, the church cannot speak for the state at all, but only individual Christians can speak anonymously for the state. Nevertheless, the church community still remains "the model and prototype of the real state" by serving as "a source of renewal for the state and the power by which the state is preserved." Indeed the "church can in no case be indifferent or neutral towards this manifestation of an order so clearly related to its mission" (157). As members of the inner circle, Christians "are also automatically members of the wider circle. They cannot halt at the boundary where the inner in our circles meet, though the work of faith, love and hope which they are under orders to perform will assume different forms on either side of the boundary" (158–59). Simply put, it is not possible for the church to be indifferent to the political order because the state's power is explicitly intertwined with the mission of the church. In this way, the church always remains part of the order of creation just as the state remains part of the order of redemption.

Whereas Barth uses the language of "intercession" in *Rechtfertigung und Recht*, here he reverts back to Barmen's language of "reminder." The church *reminds* the state of its true purpose, which is to bring honor to God. Although Barth continues the line of thinking established earlier, calling for the 'priestly role' of the church, he places a greater activist responsibly upon the church in calling the state to a particular political direction. The church continues to *be* the church through its intercessory role of being a witness to the gospel, praying and working for the good of the state, making distinctions between just and unjust governments, and declaring firmly that the state falls under God's rule. However, by "reminding" the state of its function, purpose, and hope, the church becomes more aware of its own political task. Through its own moral deliberation, the church "will choose and desire whichever seems to be the better political system in any particular situation, and in accordance with this choice and desire it will offer its support here and its resistance there." "It is in the making of such distinctions, judgments, and choices from its own centre, and in the practical decision which necessarily flows from that centre, Barth continues, that the Christian community expresses its 'subordination' to the civil community and fulfills its share of political responsibility" (162–63).

In his most concrete example of this analogous relationship between the inner circle and the outer circle, Barth develops twelve analogies between the two communities. The cornerstone of these analogies is the one Barth mentions first, namely because of the incarnation in which God stands with humanity, so too the civil community should defend the dignity and rights of humanity before serving any cause that apparently serves humanity. Humanity should not serve causes, but "causes have to serve man" (172). On this point hangs all the other analogies. Just as church gives witness to God's gracious justification, so too the civil community, along with the church, will support governments, most clearly embodied in constitutional democracies, of impartial justice. Just as Christ came to the poor and lost, so too the church should support civil governments that seek to address the needs of the poor. Just as God gives freedom to the church and state through God's gracious covenant, so too the church should reject totalitarian and authoritarian governments. Just

40

as the church is primarily a responsible community of individuals, so too the church should reject radical political individualism and collectivism. Just as the equality of Christians is established in baptism, so too it provides the basis for a political doctrine of equality of all its citizens. Just as the multiplicity of spiritual gifts within the church provide the basis for diversity, so too it provides for an understanding separation of powers in government. Just as the Word of God should be freely proclaimed in the church, so too the state should also forbid secrecy that undermines the freedom of its citizens, including freedom of speech. Just as the church, as a collective body, serves individuals within the church, so too the civil community, as a collective body, serves its citizens. Just as the church is diverse yet one, so too the civil community should relativize its boundaries and be inclusive of difference. Just as God is both a God of judgment and mercy, so too the church reminds the state that it may, as an act of last resort, engage in violence as the way to maximize peace—which remains the final word; only the state, not the church, may use force to bring about peace and justice.

Therefore, moving beyond his earlier writings, Barth argues that the state is not only a *guardian* but also a *witness* to the kingdom of God. It is true that the Christian community has no specific political "idea, system, or progamme" to give to the state as the divine form of government, but by way of reminder, it does offer a clear "direction and a line" of thinking that can be recognized and acknowledged as criterion of a 'just state.' From these analogies it is clear that Barth did not see all government systems in the same way. Not all cats are grey! Therefore, he concluded that "on the whole toward the form of State, which, if not actually realized in the so-called democracies, is at any rate more or less honestly clearly intended and desired" (182). In its freedom to obey the Word of God, "the Church makes itself responsible for the shape and reality of the civil community" by reminding the state of its own self-limitations, but also seeking to develop the most humane form of political organization possible. The Christian community must never seek to be a 'state-church', thus, seeking its own privileges or respect—as a right—in relation

41

to the state. The church never serves Christian causes but human causes. If the church finds that it has such privileges, it risks losing its freedom to "be the Church all the more," which draws it back to its central commitment to the Word of God. The church's politics is not to better itself but humanity as a whole. "If the church takes up its share of political responsibility, it must mean that it is taking that human initiative which the State cannot take; it is giving the state the impulse which it cannot give itself; it is reminding the state of those things of which it is unable to remind itself" (170). Because of its witness to the kingdom the church of stands for the welfare of human beings, not abstract causes or universalist ideas however noble and good. The "Church will always and in all circumstances be interested primarily in human beings and not some abstract cause" (171). Yet in serving humanity the church supports policies that promote what's beneficial for humanity. These include: a constitutional democracy; social and economic justice to the week and threatened; basic human rights guaranteed by the state; political equality and equal protection of all citizens under law; and the right of self-determination or the right to have freedom to engage the institutional life of society through the family, education, art, science, religion, and culture. By affirming these, the church bears witness to the state about God's purpose for humanity. Only when the state becomes committed to the human good, and not some particular cause or ideology, can it begin to resemble a "just state" (Rechtsstadt).

Barth's Later Writings and Current Discussion

In the 1950s, in the aftermath of World War II, Barth began reexamining the Pauline and Deutero-Pauline accounts of the "principalities and powers."[63] This theme, present from his earliest writings, became a larger theme in his uncompleted 'ethics of reconciliation,' which was published as *The Christian Life*.[64] Barth's task of biblical interpretation does not begin by demythologizing the text in order to make it relevant to a modern audience, but instead uses the biblical narrative to demythologize the various modern hegemonies that repress human freedom. No one was more aware of the multiple faces of hegemony than Barth, who struggled to provide a theological account of the reality of events from World War I to the Cold War. Barth's Yes to human freedom and No to absolutism rightly situate him as both a "theologian of freedom" *and* a theologian "against hegemony."[65] These "pseudo-objective" powers threaten human life, always seeking to become hegemonic and determinative of humanity's future; they are not intrinsically hegemonic, but act 'as if' they are because humanity, corrupted by its estrangement from God, infuses them with hegemonic power. In light of God's 'objective reality', they have only a "limited and relative power" because they have been defeated and "dedemonized" by Jesus Christ (215). It is the *ignorance* of the powers, both in their existence and falleness, which serves as its greatest potential threat to humanity, because even if people are able to *name* the powers, they may not seek God's deliverance from their power. In contrast, Christians are to bear witness to the fallenness of the powers by limiting and resisting their influence in the world. In their actions, Christians must be tentative and cautious, while at the same time purposeful and resolute; they must be cautious about making absolute judgments about right principles or courses of action 'against' these powers. Resistance against the powers, therefore, is fashioned primarily by the task of Christian discipleship and witness and not by one's confident dislike for the powers.[66] Standing against the powers also means positively standing *for* God's cause and good purpose in the world.

The power of political absolutism Barth calls "Leviathan." The New Testament writers were not naïve about the "political absolutisms" that "work behind and above the attitudes and acts of the great and little potentates, the highly diversified governments of the day" (219). Like them, Barth argues theological politics should not be preoccupied with political theory as such, but the "question of the demonic which is visibly at work in all politics" (219). "The demonism of politics consists in the idea of 'empire,' which is always

43

inhuman as such. This can be a monarchical, aristocratic, democratic, nationalistic, or socialistic, idea" (220). 'Empire' changes the normal or "just state" into the "marginal" or immoral state. Instead of the state serving humanity and the world, it forces humanity (and the world) to serve its own disastrous ends. Political authority, if it is to be just and right (*Recht*), must integrate power and the moral law, which are both grounded in a moral ontology that ultimately depends upon God's revelation of grace in Jesus Christ. Thus, when persons reject God's authority and say No to God's established objective order of redemption and place themselves as masters of the political realm, the "demonic" in politics emerges within human society (219). There is a fine line between the dialectical polarity between the demonic' state that denies God and the divine state that places itself above God. Both are driven by the "myth of the state" as an "earthly God", as found in the "mythical language" of the "Beast from the abyss" in Revelation 13:1-8. Barth admits that the temptation of Leviathan, the love of power and empire, remains a temptation for any society, at any time, under any system of government.[67] With the Nazi experience fresh in his mind, Barth sees Leviathan's message of Yes and No, of attraction and oppression, as linked with the implementation of a "program and structure" that promises freedom to its adherents and cruelty to its enemies. Thus, the power of Leviathan is not principally located in an evil tyrant or group of tyrants, but a totalitarian *system* or program, in which all dissenting or alternative voices are eliminated; the state, in all its power, becomes totalitarian, that is, the 'total' or 'end' of society. Any nation, with the power available, is susceptible to the temptation to replace the "might of right" with the "right of might" (221). Indeed, Barth warns that any state, including the democratic states of Western Europe and the United States, are not "immune to the tendency to become at least a little Leviathan" (221).

So, how is a Christian to resist the power of Leviathan and act responsibly in the world? Although Barth never finished his ethics of reconciliation, in which he was to give his final word about his theological politics, he did leave us with some important trajectories of thought. The Christian revolt against the 'powers' implies an active "struggling for righteousness", a struggling *for* peace, hope, and freedom (205). In themes that go back to his early writings, Barth's eschatologically-guided theological politics neither identifies nor separates human action and the kingdom of God, but places it 'along side' the kingdom; it refuses to privilege the "already" over the "not yet," or the "not yet" over the "already" (266). Christian responsibility is "kingdom like" in that it stands for the good and against evil, but without absolutizing any particular moral strategy, because to do so fosters the risk of replacing one potential hegemony with another. Barth writes:

> In this field there can be no absolute Yes or No carrying an absolute commitment. One reason for this is that an absolute guarantee of human right and worth cannot be expected from the rule of any idea or the power of any life-form. From one standpoint or another, every idea or life–form will sooner or later prove a threat to man. Hence Christians looking always to the only problem that seriously and finally interests them, must allow themselves the liberty in certain circumstances of saying only a partial Yes or No where a total one is expected, or of saying Yes today where they said No yesterday, and visa versa. Their totally definitive decision is for man and not for any cause. They will never let themselves be addressed as prisoners of their own decisions or slaves of any sacrosanct consistency. (268)

Christian political ethics must remain 'confident yet cautious' of its task in the world. Christians must remain confident in resisting the power of Leviathan and standing with the victimized, but they must also be cautious about making absolute judgments or actions of either for or against or Yes or No. In a nice summation, Barth dialectically argues that the Christian action of "Yes and No in this sphere can always be only a relative Yes and No, supremely because if it were more they would be affirming and acknowledging the existence of

45

those absolute or lordless powers, canonizing their deification, and instead of resisting the true and most dangerous enemies of man and his right, life, and work, offering them the most hazardous and fateful help" (268). Even though God invites Christians to act decisively, purposively, and confidently today against powers, that distorts God's name in the world, by seeking to embody a "little righteousness," these same Christians must move cautiously between declaring an absolute Yes and No, or for and against anything that is potentially hegemonic. Christian witness remains dialectical and *aporetic*, and it can easily degenerate into hegemonic personal or communal commitments, which become "absolute principles" instead of "theses" or reasoned arguments (268).

What then becomes the task of Christian moral responsibility in politics? In *The Christian Life*, Barth further argues that Christian moral responsibility emerges dialectically within the three relational spheres or "concentric circles" of the personal sphere or the relationship to others, the ecclesial sphere or relationship to the church, and the social sphere or one's relationship to the world. In response to God's gracious covenant, Christians remain responsible to listen and give witness to the Word of God in these three relational spheres by first invoking God's action and presence within these spheres, and then seeking ways to be faithful witnesses within them. If the divine-human dialectic provides the theory for moral responsibility, then the individual-church-world dialectic provides the arena of action in which responsible behavior takes place.

Most important for his theological politics is his discussion of the church. In *The Christian Life*, Barth draws on an earlier distinction he made in *Church Dogmatics* 4/2 of the 'secular church' of "alienation" and the 'sacral church' of "glorification."[68] In this latter work he calls the first pole, the "church in defect" and the second the "church of excess." These two poles, of course, are but two sides of the same coin as they both seek the "self-preservation" of the church. The first pole is a 'secularized church' that fails to distinguish itself from the various ideologies of the world. Barth rejects the "church in defect" or the 'secular church' because it too easily

46

accommodates itself to the surrounding culture with little critical distance. Unlike the accommodationist church, which denies the importance of God's Word, the "church of excess" remains supremely overconfident and arrogant of its knowledge of God. As a "holy church" it equates its own "form and action," its traditions and practices, with that of the Word of God. "*It* speaks his truth; *it* extends or denies his grace; *it* proclaims his law" (137). As an "introverted church" it is more preoccupied with *itself* than with the "Living Lord" that it serves; "it is primarily interested in itself, and in its Lord only for its own sake" (136). Moreover, as an "infallible church" it is supremely zealous to 'be the church', but it often becomes misguided and confused of its own mission and purpose. In doing so, it obscures the Word of God and denies God's freedom to both reconcile and pronounce judgment on the church. "How can God be confessed," asks Barth, "when his Word is not free but bound" and "when ostensibly to greater glory of God it is bound to the church?'" (137). In short, the 'church in excess' is a "presumptuous church which exalts and puffs itself up" (136).

Moreover, like the 'secular church, the second 'holy church avoids listening and bearing witness to the Word by replacing it with some other word, but unlike the first extreme, this church prioritizes itself and its 'religion' over the world and the individual person. It too sees the growing secularization of the world, but tries to overcome the tension between the church and world by triumphing *over* the world. This church seeks to remove itself from the world by isolating itself from the needs and voices of others; it seeks its own "self-preservation." More dramatically, it even becomes resentful and antagonistic toward the secular *other*. By overvaluing the church it undervalues the individual person and the world. Indeed, by obscuring the Word of God with 'church-speak' it invariably distorts its relation to outsiders and the world, by denying that the World of God may speak there as well in its "secular parables." It too, in the end, fails to "give precedence to the Word" and instead gives precedence to the *church*. Instead of saying *No* to non-Christian viewpoints, therefore, Barth advises Christians to "listen to all other ethics

47

insofar as it has to receive from them at every point the material for its own deliberations. To that extent its attitude to every other ethics is not negative but comprehensive."[69] When Christian moral discourse loses its comprehensiveness and becomes *esoteric*, it becomes parochial and isolated from other voices in the world at large. "Why should it not be possible for God to raise up witnesses from this world of tarnished untruth," Barth asks, "so that true words are uttered and heard even where it might seem that at very best no more than crude or refined deception may be expected?"[70] When Christians prohibit listening to the Word in and through the voice of the *other* in "secular parables", they refuse to allow the Word of God to "illumine, accentuate, or explain the biblical witness in a particular time and situation."[71]

As stated in the beginning of this essay, Barth's theological politics has many similarities to the 'emergent tradition' of recent years, as found in the thought of Oliver O'Donovan, John Milbank, Stanley Hauerwas, and John Howard Yoder. Daniel Bell, Jr., argues that the emergent tradition challenges the "modern nation-state's claim to the right to organize human community in its own image," and instead begins with the church as a political community in its own right. "This is to say," continues Bell, "the emergent tradition finds the political correlate of the Christian *mythos*, not in the secular state and civil society, but in the church."[72] In the conclusion of this essay, therefore, it may be helpful in very briefly explaining some differences between the emergent tradition and Barth, as a way to further argue why Barth's theological politics makes a difference today. Each of these theologians is quite successful in his own right in shifting Christian political thought from a social-science driven political theology to a theologically-driven theological politics. In this way, they share Barth's basic premise of beginning with a theological description of reality. Yet there are crucial differences between Barth and these other thinkers on the issue of church and state, and the dialectic of church/world or church/culture in *relation* to church and state. Most basically, unlike Barth, the ecclesial-centered approach of the emergent tradition repeatedly loops back to the social and political nature of the Christian community and not to the Word of God, which transcends the church. This raises important questions about how church and state/culture/world ought to be identified, distinguished, and related.

We begin first with John Howard Yoder, who of the four remains the most influenced by Barth's theology. Like Barth, Yoder sees the church's positive task as bearing witness to the state, yet unlike him, and more like others in the emergent tradition, Yoder places a stronger *diastasis* between church and state. This is most obvious in Yoder's repeated discussion of the heresy of "Constantinianism" and its impact on the church, in particular through the legacy of Christendom.[73] This heresy has continued into the post-Christendom era in many forms in which the church is corrupted by the *ethos* of the state, society, or culture. This leads Yoder to be critical of Barth's use of analogy in the "Christian Community and the Civil Community," but more appreciative of his analogy of church and civil law in *Church Dogmatics* IV/2.[74] In the first analogy, Yoder argues that Barth seems more interested in demonstrating the Christian basis for "civic virtues" and "human rights" of the bourgeois liberal democratic state than explicating actual practices of the church. In this later work, however, Barth is more interested with explicating the 'public' nature of church law, whether or not, it finds a home in liberal democratic polity.[75] Yoder dislikes Barth's first analogy because he sees it going from the world to the church, whereas the latter analogy goes from the church to the world. Yoder, above all, is concerned that the analogy be faithful to the New Testament practices of the church, for only then can it be a proper basis for Christian ethics.[76] The church—not the state—remains the visible reminder or 'sign' of the kingdom's reality, promise, and hope.

Although Yoder and Barth would agree that the state is a guardian, they part company on whether the state, more positively, is a *witness* to the Kingdom of God. For Yoder the *esse* of the state is a 'fallen power' who continues to wreak havoc in the world and is characterized by the use of coercion and force. The state cannot be the outer circle of the kingdom of God for Yoder, because as a fallen power, it is opposed to

49

the way of peace and justice, thus, whatever connection the state has to the kingdom, it has through its relationship to the church. As a distinct society from the state (and world), the church gives a distinct pacifist witness to the church's "messianic politics." For Yoder, God uses the state, as guardian, as part fallen creation, to restrain chaos and control evil, but for Barth, God can use the state as witness to the kingdom. Even the most tyrannical state still remains under God's redemption.[77] We may recall that for Barth the Christian belongs to herself, the church, *and* the world. The Christian does not *choose* to be in solidarity with the world, says Barth, but "is in solidarity with it from the very first."[78] In contrast, Yoder's distinction between church and state tends toward separation—not dialectical relation—under Christ's rule.

In contrast to Yoder and more like Barth, O'Donovan presents a positive doctrine of the state and a well-developed argument for Christian political responsibility within the state. Yet, more than Barth, O'Donovan remains a defender of the 'Christian state' and legacy of Christendom. "So," says O'Donovan, "without appealing to any notion of Christian state or state-within-the-church, Barth makes the state as such a witness to Christ's rule. But how can it witness to what it has not heard?"[79] O'Donovan reasons that Barth's post-Christendom description of the church allows for the independent secular state, but does little to explain how this secular state 'remembers' itself without appealing to some notion of Christendom. Similarity to Yoder, Barth argues that the state's secularity has 'freed' the church to give witness to the Word of God. Yet unlike Yoder (and O'Donovan), Barth argues that the 'secular state' ought to be respected in its own right, because it too has been redeemed, as the 'outer circle', within the kingdom of God. For Barth, the value of the *secular* is more than its 'passing away', as it is with O'Donovan. Barth places more emphasis on the value of *otherness* and secularity in its own right; Christians must "eavesdrop in the world at large" because this too has been redeemed in Jesus Christ.[80]

50

The others in the emergent tradition, namely Hauerwas and Milbank, remain even more contrastive, rather than dialectical, in their relation of church and state (and world). In this way, Barth remains closer to the thought of O'Donovan and Yoder than he does to Hauerwas and Milbank. For these latter theologians, the church remains not only an alternative *polis* to the communities of the world, but also the only authentic *polis* within the world. What theology says about other societies or communities emerges from the particular society of the church. For example, Christian social theory, says Milbank, is "first and foremost an *ecclesiology,* and only an account of other human societies to the extent that the Church defines itself, in its practice as in continuity and discontinuity with these [other] societies." Indeed, he adds, "There can only be a distinguishable Christian social theory because there is also a distinguishable Christian mode of action, a definite practice." [81] Likewise, Hauerwas claims, "the social significance of the church [is] as a distinct society with integrity peculiar to itself." "The church," Hauerwas adds, "does not exist to provide an ethos for democracy or any other form of social organization, but stands as a political alterative to every nation, witnessing to the kind of social life possible for those that have been formed by the story of Christ." [82] Theological politics begins with the 'social life' of the church as a 'distinct society', with its particular practices, character, and virtues as a way to identify the Christian way.

Unlike Barth's centrality on the Word of God, this ecclesial-centered view comes close to linking the moral ontology of Christian ethics with the moral *ethos* of the church, that is with its practices and its pedagogical character. John Webster perceptively warns that an ecclesial-centered theology and ethics "runs the risk of not making sufficiently clear the distinction in kind between 'church' and 'sociality', so that church comes to be a cultural and not a theological concept."[83] Webster repeats Barth's claim that there must be a *diastasis* between the Word of God and the church, just as there is between the Word of God and the world; however, there is no substantive diastasis between the church and the world, which remain dialectically linked under the authority of

51

the Word of God.[84] Moreover, the privileging of the church over the other two spheres (individual and world) of Christian existence inevitably *undervalues* persons and the world. This leads to resentment against persons and communities outside the church, denying that the Word of God has also come to them. Regarding this point, Jeffrey Stout claims the "new traditionalism" of Milbank and Hauerwas presumes a hidden non-theological commitment to an "ideological expression of the enclave society."[85] What makes their theology problematic is not their particularism or single-minded commitment to a moral tradition like Christianity, but their 'resentment' of the secular. It is no coincidence that Stout relies on Barth's theology when he argues that the "secular world is not to be feared or merely refused by anyone committed to charity and justice in dealing with others. It is rather an arena in which a Christian can hope to proclaim God's word and observe the transfiguring effects of God's love on the lives of his creatures."[86] By continuously 'looping-back' to the church instead of the Word, and privileging the ecclesial sphere over the personal and worldly spheres, the emergent tradition makes theological politics insufficiently dialectical and aporetic. This move not only endangers the risk of an ecclesial hegemony (i.e., 'church in excess') and resentment against the *other*, but worse yet, displacing the Word from its privileged status in Christian ethics. Both the human and divine *other* can potentially become marginalized.

Barth's dialectical theology makes a difference today because like the representatives of the emergent tradition, he sees the church bearing witness to God's declarative Yes to the world, but unlike them, he also refuses to stand *against* the secular world simply because of its secularity or its *otherness*. Barth avoids two extreme positions of the church-world dialectic: 1) by stressing the *homogeneity* of the world to the church (and individuals), Christians inevitably endorse a kind of 'Christian secularism' or 'secular Christianity'; and 2) by stressing the *otherness* of the world, Christians create a false separation between themselves (and the church) and the world, which leads to the exclusion of the world. For our purposes, the 'emergent tradition' moves close to the second error of

52

stressing the *otherness* of the world, in such a way that Christians stand 'against' the world, while standing 'for' the church.[87] Barth's theology provides a dialectical path between 'homogeneity' and 'otherness', which allows the church to value the 'secular' but not the hegemony of secularism. An ecclesial-centered ethics has difficulty valuing the secularity because it begins, not with the Word of God, but with the 'social reality' of the church as *polis*, which remains the visible body of Christ on earth. Although Barth maintains that Christians, as Christ's body on earth, should strive to maintain their particular identity in the world as witnesses to God's Word, this identity is dialectically linked with the other two spheres of personal and worldly existence, which stand under the authority of the Word. This affirms the priority of the Word of God and respect and responsibility 'to' and 'for' others and the world.

Barth's dialectical thought avoids the extremes of the 'demonic' and 'divine' views of the state and rather sees the state as a secular institution, redeemed by Jesus Christ, and able to give witness to God's kingdom in the world. Both the church and state belong to God's kingdom, which means the church serves the state by 'being the church' and the state serves the church by 'being the state.' Although Christians should reject all political ideologies, including democracy and liberalism, as contingent upon Christian belief, he does argue that constitutional democracy remains the best form of government so far discovered. Barth does not see the church as an alternative *polis* to the state, which is dominated by the hegemony of secularism. In Barth's view, there is only one polis, one kingdom of God, of which the church is the inner circle and the state is the outer circle. The church and state are differentiated but not separated, nor is the church more 'graced' than the state in relation to the kingdom of God. To withhold God's redemptive grace from the civil community is to declare the state (and society) as demonic. Barth rejects this idea because Christ remains both the head of the church *and* state, which enables Christians to stand in dialectical relationship of solidarity *with* the secular democratic state. This makes it further possible for Christians to stand for so-called secular theories like political liberalism or an inclusive democracy. Both the church and the state are capable of oppressive activity, because they are often driven by sinful human interests; so too, they are both reconciled and redeemed by God's covenant of grace. A democratic state must be preferred to all other conceptions of political authority because it stands with and for the dignity of persons, a friendly separation of church from the state, and various human rights.

Barth's position also stands in contrast to those who uncritically view the state as redemptive or the 'divine state'. This view creates a *synthesis* between church and state. There is no doubt that Barth would share this concern as would the emergent tradition, who, above all, is cognizant of the risks associated with the church's accommodation to secular culture. This latter synthesis position—what H. Richard Niebuhr calls the "Christ of culture" position, is known as the 'Eusebian temptation', or in its worst form Yoder's "Constantinianism"—presumes the Kingdom of God is revealed in and through the state's action in history. Barth's rejection of both Nazism, as well as his criticism of the Western anti-communism of the 1950s, follows from this ideological identification of God's redemptive purposes with the purposes of the state. Regardless if it's the view of civil religion or a fictitious 'Christian state', religion and the state become too closely identified with each other; the state becomes the church or the church becomes the state. In either case, the state loses it secularity and becomes a divine state. This temptation, no doubt, remains a risk for any democratic society, especially if that society has great military and economic power, like the United States. Some theologians, including lesser-known Abraham Lincoln in the second Inaugural address, have long been concerned with too closely identifying America's mission in the world with the Word of God. Inquiring into the subject of whether and how this view may be evident in American politics and culture more generally today, especially in the rhetoric of the Christian Right, goes well beyond this essay. Yet from Barth we may surmise that the important question today is: what does it mean to be the confessing church today in America? Although

54

differences may emerge in how this questioned is answered, it's the question itself that remains the most important issue here, and that is precisely why Barth's theology still makes a difference.

Endnotes

[1] Will Herberg, "The Social Philosophy of Karl Barth," in Karl Barth, *Community, State, and Church: Three Essays* (Glousester, Mass.: Peter Smith, 1968) 11–67. Perhaps the most useful portion of Herberg's essay was his concise, yet comprehensive, discussion of the two main Christian traditions of the state, and Barth's departure from them. The first 'natural law' tradition begins with the premise that humans are social and political creatures who are rationally constituted in such a way that they seek their own flourishing within a social and communal order; the state, or civil community, is a natural extension of humanity's communal nature, in which persons seek to live, flourish, and promote the common good. God creates natural law as a physical, moral, and spiritual order that is discernable through human reason, and used by the state to promote human virtue, culture, and reason. This tradition, of course, is primarily linked with the Thomistic tradition and the Roman Catholic church, but has also been found intermittently in various Protestant traditions, particularly the Anglican church in the modern period. In contrast is the "Augustinian-Reformation" tradition, which serves as the basis for most Protestant thought. Although this tradition is rooted more in Scripture, the Church Fathers, and Stoicism, it finds it first major development in St. Augustine. Beginning with a more keen sense of the power of personal and public sinfulness, this view remains less confident that the state promotes what is best for the human community. Therefore, the most important function of the state is to provide protection or preservation of what is good in the human community. This view prefers to see the state as an 'order of creation' or 'order of preservation' rather than a 'natural' order. Herberg rightly demonstrates how Barth departs from both of these views and places the state under the order of redemption rather than under 'creation' or 'natural law.' This 'Christocentric' theme, Herberg argues, is most fully developed in Barth's essay, "The Civil Community and the Christian Community," but is also found in a less developed form in "Church and State" and "Gospel and Law." On all these points Herberg is useful; however, he fails to see how Barth's thought in these three essays relates to his earlier *and* later thought.

[2] John Howard Yoder, *Karl Barth and the Problem of War and Other Essays on Barth*, edited with foreword by Mark Thiessen Nation, (Eugene, Ore.: Cascade Books, 2003) 93. This reprint of Yoder's 1970 book includes several other essays by Yoder on Barth written from 1963–1994.

[3] Fredrich-Willhelm Marquardt, *Theologie und Sozialismus: Das Beispiel Karl Barths* (Munich: Chr.Kaiser Verlag 1972). George Hunsinger collected several important essays by Marquardt and others pertaining to Barth's

socialism and politics. See George Hunsinger, *Karl Barth and Radical Politics* (Philadelphia: Westminster, 1976).

[4] Timothy Gorringe, *Karl Barth: Against Hegemony* (Oxford and New York: Oxford University Press, 1999).

[5] For important introductions to Barth's theological ethics, see Nigel Biggar, *The Hastening that Waits: Karl Barth's Ethics* (New York: Oxford University Press, 1993) and the works by John Webster: John Webster, *Barth's Ethics of Reconciliation* (Cambridge: Cambridge University Press, 1995) and J. Webster, *Barth's Moral Theology: Human Action in Barth's Thought* (Grand Rapids: Eerdmans, 1998). For concise introductions to Barth's political thought, see William Werpehowski, "Karl Barth and Politics" in John Webster, (ed.) *The Cambridge Companion to Karl Barth* (Cambridge: Cambridge University Press, 2000) 228–42. See also Hadden Willmer's "Karl Barth" in Peter Scott and William T. Cavanaugh's (eds.) *The Blackwell Companion to Political Theology* (Oxford: Blackwell, 2004) 123–35. For a good discussion of Barth theology of the state in light of the Barmen Declaration, see Eberhard Jüngel, *Christ, Justice, and Peace: Toward a Theology of the State in Dialogue with the Barmen Declaration*, trans. by D. Bruce Hamill and Alan J. Torrance, (Edinburgh: T & T Clark, 1992).

[6] Frank Jehle, *Ever Against the Stream: The Politics of Karl Barth, 1906–1968*. Translated by Richard and Martha Burnett, (Grand Rapids: Eerdmans, 2002).

[7] Alan J. Torrance, "Introductory Essay" in Eberhard Jüngel, *Christ, Justice, and Peace*, xx.

[8] Daniel Bell, Jr., argues for a similar distinction between the "dominant tradition" and the "emergent tradition" in political theology. The former group includes European political theology, in the manner of Johann Baptist Metz and Jürgen Moltmann, Latin American liberation theology, in the manner of Leonardo Boff and Gustavo Gutiérrez, various versions of American feminist, womanist, and African-American (Black) theologies, and various types of public theology, *a la* Max Stackhouse and Richard John Neuhaus. The latter group, seeking to develop a 'theological politics' like Barth's, includes John Howard Yoder, Stanley Hauerwas, John Milbank, and Oliver O'Donovan. Interestingly, Bell does not refer to Barth in this essay, even though Barth's influence upon the emergent tradition is apparent. See, Daniel M. Bell, Jr., "State and Civil Society" in Scott and Cavanaugh's (eds.) *The Blackwell Companion to Political Theology*, 423–48.

[9] F. Jehle, *Ever Against the Stream*, 44.

[10] Barth's view of war and the state has been one of the more debated issues in his political ethics. In addition to the works mentioned above (particularly Yoder's), see Rowan Williams, "Barth, War, and the State," in Nigel Biggar, (ed.) *Reckoning With Barth* (Oxford: Mowbray, 1988) 170–97 ; and Oliver O'Donovan, "Karl Barth and Paul Ramsey's Use of Power," in Oliver O'Donovan and Joan Lockwood O'Donovan, *Bonds of Perfection: Christian Politics, Past and Present* (Grand Rapids: Eerdmans, 2004) 246–75. Suffice it to say, Yoder, the pacifist, is critical of Barth's apparent 'just war' stance, and O'Donovan, the 'just war' theorist, is critical of Barth's practical pacifism. Williams remains both appreciative and critical of Barth's apparent "unfinished" ethic. Almost all scholars who write on Barth's ethics have addressed this issue in their writings. Even though Barth's thought remains in constant movement, there is a consistent line that remains throughout. William Werpehowski sums this up nicely when he says that Barth's practical pacifism "can connect evangelical politics and political realities by limiting war to its proper purpose, and extending political power's use short of war to effect forms of peace that meet more nearly the measure of creaturely humanity" (W. Werpehowski, "Karl Barth and Politics," 240.)

[11] The state's commitment to 'peacemaking' suspends discussion of the state's use of force, and rightly shifts the focus to strategies for implementing justice and peace. Glen Stassen's work on "just peacemaking" has been a useful contribution in this debate, as he has argued there are three positions—not two (namely, the just war and pacifist positions)—in Christian ethics, but there is also the middle position of 'just peacemaking'. Christians who support this third position are more concerned with discussion about how to 'prevent war' rather than whether war ought to be seen as just or unjust. However, when war actually starts, Christians must either move toward a 'just war' or 'pacifist' view. See Glen Stassen and David Gushee, *Kingdom Ethics: Following Jesus in Contemporary Context* (Downers Grove: InterVarsity, 2003) 174. For earlier discussions of 'just peacemaking', see Glen Stassen, *Just Peacemaking: Transforming Initiatives for Justice and Peace* (Louisville, Ky.: Westminster John Knox, 1992) and G. Stassen, (ed.) *Just Peacemaking: Ten Practices for Abolishing War* (Cleveland: Pilgrim, 1998).

[12] For the best and most comprehensive overview of Barth's political life, see Eberhard Busch, *Karl Barth: His Life From Letters and Autobiographical Texts*, trans. by John Bowden, (Philadelphia: Fortress, 1976) and Frank Jehle, *Ever Against the Stream*.

[13] One of the early writings from this period is the 1911 speech, "Jesus Christ and the Social Movement." Combining theological liberalism and socialism, Barth argues that Jesus sought to address needs of the poor through the establishment of the Kingdom of God on earth. This included

developing a community of 'comrades' committed to these principles, and abolishing the greed associated with the quest for more private property. See K. Barth, "Jesus Christ and the Social Movement," in George Hunsinger, *Karl Barth and Radical Politics*, 19–45.

[14] In his fine book examining Barth's early thought, Bruce McCormack examines Barth's sermons of 1913–14, leading up to the Great War, and argues that he began departing from liberal theology in the following areas: 1) he placed more emphasis on divine judgment and the reality of human sinfulness; 2) he developed a critical stance toward 'Religion' as understood by liberal theology; 3) he began addressing God as "wholly other" from humanity; and 4) he saw the kingdom of God as divinely ordained and not ushered in through human efforts or movements like Religious Socialism. Bruce McCormack, *Karl Barth's Critically Realistic Dialectical Theology: Its Genesis and Development*, 1909–1936, (Oxford: Clarendon, 1995) 92–104.

[15] K. Barth, "The Righteousness of God" in *The Word of God and the Word of Man* (New York: Harper & Row, 1957) 24.

[16] McCormack argues that Barth's theology is 'critical' in that it generally accepts Kant's critique of metaphysics, which posits that there "is no epistemological way that leads from the empirical world to the divine source." It is also 'realist' in that God is the "reality which is complete and whole in itself apart from and prior to the knowing activity of human individuals." B. McCormack, *Karl Barth's Critically Realistic Dialectical Theology*, 129–30.

[17] Moreover, although Ragaz appreciated Karl Marx's analysis of capitalism, he rejected Marx's atheistic dialectical materialism and class revolution, and sought rather to 'Christianize' the socialist movement, thus ushering in God's kingdom. In contrast, Kutter was a more firmly committed Marxist and German Nationalist than Ragaz, yet he insisted that 'publicly' the church's task should not confuse its message of social justice with the secular movements of socialism, and instead it must faithfully 'wait' for God's action. When the Great War erupted, Kutter strongly defended the German cause, believing it to be possibly linked with the providential movement of God's Spirit in history, whereas Ragaz opposed both the violence of war and political nationalism, both of which were contradictory to a worldwide Religious Socialist movement. From Kutter's view, Ragaz was engaged in the impossibility of Christianizing the movement, and, with it, losing the central core teaching of the kingdom of God. From Ragaz's view, Kutter's theology of human action and politics was wrongly grounded in a quietist or sectarian divorce of theology from politics, which essentially made him a theological dreamer.

[18] What Barth found appealing in Christoph Blumhardt was a theologically credible compromise between Ragaz and Kutter. So unlike Ragaz's 'hastening' position, Blumhardt's belief in the eschatological hope of a new world was directly linked to God's divine action rather than human progress through Religious Socialism. Moreover, unlike Kutter's 'waiting' position, Blumhardt did have an active role in the practical side of politics. What Blumhardt did for Barth is allow him to envision the hope of the gospel in light of God's eschatological action in Jesus Christ. Before this change Barth was preoccupied with the human movement of Religious Socialism *itself*, instead of God's movement in history. Barth needed to begin his thinking in a different place and 'take God seriously', which opened himself up to the transcendent otherness and mystery of God.

[19] These essays are found in Karl Barth, *The Word of God and the Word of Man*, trans. by Douglas Horton, (New York: Harper & Row, 1957) 9–27; 28–50.

[20] For a detailed discussion of these points in *Romans 1*, see B. McCormack, *Karl Barth's Critically Realistic Dialectical Theology*, pp. 135–83. Barth uses the Pauline text to argue against idealistic conceptions of ethics that posit principles of the 'good' without considering human sinfulness and God's righteousness. A Christian ethics is not located in the divine law, but is found in a person's *immediate* connection to God, through being in Christ's body, which enables the Christian to live in freedom within each moment. This freedom does not come at the expense of responsibility, however. It is not Antinomian because Paul admonishes the Christian toward moral "exhortation," which means practicing love and justice toward others and resisting legitimate authority. Still, he admits there are "confused situations," like the "dirty businesses" of politics, where one is often powerless to do what is good or left with no options except sinful ones. Even in this early writing, Barth is attempting to go beyond the traditional law-gospel dialectic, which will be fully developed in the 1935 essay, "Gospel and Law."

[21] K. Barth, "The Christian's Place in Society," in *The Word of God and the Word of Man.*, 272–327. Because the Christian in society is really "Christ in us" in society, this forces Christians to look at *divine* action, which reveals that God is *with* us, but also "over us, behind us and beyond us" (274). Christians should never assume that through their "criticizing, protesting, reforming, organizing, democratizing, socializing, and revolutionizing—*however fundamental and thoroughgoing these may be*—we satisfy the ideal of the kingdom of God" (320). The remainder of references to this text will be noted in the text by parentheses.

[22] K. Barth, *The Epistle to the Romans*, 2nd edition, (Oxford: Oxford University Press, 1933) 455.

[23] K. Barth, *Ethics* (New York: Seabury, 1981).

[24] Although Barth had many theological critics who shared his politics, like Rudolph Bultmann, Paul Tillich, and Emil Brunner, there were also many who appreciated his theology but disagreed with his politics, including supporters of the 'two kingdoms' theology within the Confessing Church. There were others, like the confessionalist Lutheran theologian Paul Althaus, who claimed that Barth's faulty theology paved the way for his misguided politics. Prior to Hitler's rise to power, Althaus became critical of Barth's support for the Weimar's liberal constitutional state, and welcomed a return to 'law and order' and a surrogate return to the glorious age of the German monarch, propagated by the Nazi regime. Althaus rigorously defended the 'two kingdoms' theory, which neatly separated church and state and law and gospel into two separate realms. Althaus' theology demonstrates the inadequacy of the Lutheran doctrine of the 'two kingdoms' to respond to the Nazi rise to power. Yet it is misguided to assume that Martin Luther's position, or all Lutheranism for that matter, leads unilaterally to Christian political inactivity, or that it can be blamed for the atrocities of the Nazi regime. However, the point remains that during the 1930s in Germany, the dominance of a particular version of Luther's doctrine of the two kingdoms prevailed in the church, and with it a particular social and cultural understanding of the relationship of church and state. Theologically the central difference as Barth saw it was over how the doctrine of revelation was affected by the dialectic of law and gospel and its impact on natural theology.

[25] K. Barth, *Against the Stream: Shorter Post-War Writings 1946–52* (New York: Philosophical Library, 1954). The remainder of references to this text will be noted in the text by parentheses.

[26] K. Barth, *The Christian Life*, trans. Geoffrey W. Bromiley, (Grand Rapids: Eerdmans, 1981) 221.

[27] Quoted in John Howard Yoder, *Karl Barth and the Problem of War and Other Essays*, 102.

[28] K. Barth, *Final Testimonies,* (ed.) Eberhard Busch, trans. by G. W. Bromiley (Grand Rapids: Eerdmans, 1977) 34–35.

[29] The important earlier work here is the 1951 book on Barth, written by Hans Urs von Balthasar. H. U. von Balthasar, *The Theology of Karl Barth*, trans. E. T. Oakes, SJ (San Francisco: Ignatius, 1992). The latter view is developed in B. McCormack, *Karl Barth's Critically Realistic Dialectical Theology*. For a brief discussion of these matters see John Webster, *Barth* (New York and London: Continuum, 2000) 22–24.

[30] In addition to his lectures on *Ethics*, as previously noted, see his 1922 lectures on Calvin: K. Barth, *The Theology of John Calvin*, trans. Geoffrey W. Bromiley (Grand Rapids: Eerdmans, 1995). His 1923 lectures on the Reformed confessions: Karl Barth, *The Theology of the Reformed Confessions*, trans. Darrell L. and Judith Guder (Louisville: Westminster John Knox, 2002). And his 1924 lectures on dogmatics: K. Barth, *The Göttingen Dogmatics: Instruction in the Christian Religion* trans. Geoffrey W. Bromiley (Grand Rapids: Eerdmans, 1991).

[31] After 1924, Barth's theology became more Christologically grounded, when he discovered the Reformed doctrines of *anhypostasis* and *enhypostasis*.. "The anhypostatic-enhypostatic model was well suited for clarifying what was at stake in speaking of revelation as revelation in concealment, as indirect communication. For the Subject of this revelation is the Person of the Logos who is veiled Himself in human flesh." B. McCormack, *Karl Barth's Critically Realistic Dialectical Theology*, 362.

[32] K. Barth, *The Word of God and the Word of Man*, 186.

[33] No doubt Barth learned much from the writing of his Calvin lectures delivered that same year, in which Calvin's argumentation includes the vertical dialectical movement from point to counterpoint, from human inability to know God to God's revelation. Calvin's theology discloses a mystery of God that can never be systemized or synthesized into neat formulas. It was this background that helped his discussion of theology as a 'dialectical science'.

[34] K. Barth, *The Word of God and the Word of Man*, 172.

[35] B. McCormack, *Karl Barth's Critically Realistic Dialectical Theology*, 345.

[36] This thesis is explicated fully in the excellent book, Paul Louis Metzger, *The Word of Christ and the Word of Culture: Sacred and Secular in the Thought of Karl Barth* (Grand Rapids: Eerdmans, 2003).

[37] K. Barth, "Church and Culture," in *Theology and Church: Shorter Writings, 1920–28*, with an introduction by T. F. Torrance, trans. Louise Pettibone Smith (New York: Harper & Row, 1962) 344.

[38] Paul Metzger writes, "The question is not *whether* a synthesis between Word and world is to be ventured, but rather *how*. As in Christology proper, so too, here, it is crucial to engage the world of culture not from below, but from above, proceeding downward. As the divine Word takes to himself a potential human nature in incarnation, so too, Barth's theology of the Word

becomes a theology for the world, and its own way, a worldly theology." P. L. Metzger, *The Word of Christ and the Word of Culture*, 81.

[39] "Apologetics in this case would be the attempt to establish and justify the theologico-ethical inquiry within the framework and on the foundation of the presumptions and methods of non-theological, of wholly human thinking and language." K. Barth, *Church Dogmatics*, II/2, (Edinburgh: T&T Clark, 1957) 520. The problem, of course, is that when theology becomes principally "apologetic" it becomes reduced or absorbed into the more general non-theological frameworks. This is why Barth remained so committed to the dogmatic task of theology. Indeed, except for an occasional reference to a philosophical or literary figure, he refuses to draw upon non-theological sources into his own work. This makes it appear to the casual reader of Barth that he is opposed to any lengthy use of non-theological sources in Christian ethics, however, this is a misguided assumption as we shall see later on in this essay.

[40] The following references to *Der Römerbrief* are taken from Frank Jehle's, *Ever Against The Stream*, pp. 36–45. For original text see, K. Barth, *Der Römerbrief* (Erse Fassung) 1919, (ed.) by Herman Schmidt (Zurch: TVZ, 1985). The remainder of references to *Romans I* will be noted in the text by parentheses.

[41] In this light, Barth defines the "powerful state of the present . . . as evil in itself" and "as diametrically opposed to God's intentions" (501). More emphatically, "*all* politics as the struggle for power, as the devilish art of winning elections, is *fundamentally* dirty" (502). So, in this way, Christians should "have nothing to do with monarchies, capitalism, militarism, patriotism and political liberalism" (508). Indeed, the "divine may not be politicized and that which is human may not be divinized, not even in favor of democracy and social democracy" (509).

[42] K. Barth, "The Christian's Place in Society" in *The Word of God and the Word of Man*, 320. The remainder of references to this article will be noted in the text by parentheses.

[43] The central problem in *Romans II*, says McCormack, was "how can God make Himself known to human beings without ceasing—at any point in the process of Self-communication—to be the Subject of revelation?" This problem Barth solved by developing more futurist-orientated "consistent eschatology" in contrast to the more liberal past/present-orientated "process eschatology" of *Romans I*. This shift in eschatology leads Barth to unleash a more vibrant diastasis between a modern liberal theology and idealistic ethics and a strictly theological ethics that begins with divine actions of judgment and grace. *B. McCormack, Karl Barth's Critically Realistic Dialectical Theology*, 209–40.

[44] K. Barth, *The Epistle to the Romans*, 2nd edition, (Oxford: Oxford University Press, 1933) 430.

[45] Although revolutionary politics is closer to the Christian aspirations for justice, it is more dangerous because it believes its action is right to the extent of excluding, even hating others; such stands in contrast to forgiveness and love as found in the gospel. Like earlier writings, he is not as much interested in forging a positive politics of Christian citizenship, but to unmask the ideologies of power politics. The basis of theological politics grounded in love of the 'other' and not in Christian justifications for the politics of the left or the right. Even more than in the first edition, the second edition places God's judgment against *all* human structures and organizations.

[46] K. Barth, *The Epistle to the Romans*, 2nd edition, 431ff.

[47] Barth reverses the modern paradigm of *praxis*, which privileges ethics over theology, and instead views ethics as an inseparable part of dogmatic theology. This move leads to an understanding of moral self, not as autonomous, but one deeply *related* to God. This relation first reveals the *diastasis* of the moral subject from God, but this de-centering leads not to the "loss of the self" but to a 'transformed self', embodying an ethics of mutual correction, grounded in divine justification and forgiveness. Regarding this point, he writes: "The discovery of the One in the other can occur only as each single individual is confronted by the particular concrete others," Ibid., 476. This theme of responsibility for the other, developed more fully in his *Ethics* lectures, places the concrete *other* before us, as a disclosure of the otherness of God.

[48] K. Barth, *Ethics* (New York: Seabury, 1981). The remainder of references to this article will be noted in the text by parenthesis.

[49] J. Webster, *Barth's Moral Theology*, p. 42. Webster further writes: "Like those philosophical figures, Barth does not make interiority fundamental to what it means to be human. One of the most important themes of the *Ethics* lectures is Barth's persistent refusal to allow that moral consciousness is basic" (42).

[50] Barth's Trinitarian conception of ethics is first expressed in his 'ethics of creation', where God gives a "command of life," which is often heard within the various "callings" and "orders" of our lives. Humanity is not only a creature situated within creation, but is also a 'reconciled sinner', whose life has been altered by God the Reconciler. God's reconciliation is a repeating theme in *Ethics*, a kind of entry point into his theological ethics as a whole, which begins with the reconciling divine action in God's Word. God's

reconciling "command of law" is known in "authority," whose content is expressed in "humility," and fulfilled in "love." It is true that Barth's understanding of law and gospel had not yet developed to the place where Gospel comes before the Law, as it had in his later essay, "Gospel and Law." Nevertheless, he radically departs from traditional 'natural law', 'two kingdoms', or 'orders of creation' perspectives by placing the state and civil society within the relationship of the reconciling covenant of God and within the commitment of responsibility for the *other*.

[51] Unlike many Christian ethicists today who criticize the modern autonomous self by proposing a model of the 'social self' or 'relational self', whose character is shaped by absorption within the *ethos* of the church, Barth's theological reframing of the relational self is shaped first by the vertical disruption of the Word of God, which establishes relational dependency upon God. This is not to say that Barth avoids the question of how socio-cultural and historical forces shape the moral self, as in fact he does, which further demonstrates how he departs from the language of the unattached 'unencumbered' autonomous modern self.

[52] Hence, revolution is only possible when the state can no longer accomplish its tasks; it is possible only as an act of "last resort" within "extreme and vary rare circumstances," Barth, *Ethics*, 446. Of course, it is possible for the state to be corrupted, for the "good state" or "humble state" to become preoccupied with its own national interest, and contradict its "very nature as an order in service to its neighbor" (449). Not unlike the individual sinner, the state is fallen, but, like the sinner, God's mercy extends to the state through God's reconciliation through Christ. Therefore, the church is subject to the state as the "guardian of society" when it fulfills its divine mandate to serve and protect the community from the 'powers' that seek to undermine its commitment to humanity's welfare. But when the state no longer accepts its "co-responsibility" in humanity's service, the church "will move on to protest against the state" (450).

[53] This new translation of the Barmen Declaration (1984) can be found in the introduction to Eberhard Jüngel, *Christ, Justice, and Peace*, p. xxviii.

[54] Quoted from Arthur Cochrane, *The Church's Confession Under Hitler* (Philadelphia: Westminster, 1962) 191.

[55] Ibid.

[56] Barth's final discussion of the errors of natural theology is found in *Church Dogmatics* II/1, which was written in 1939. In Barth's summary, there are three principal errors of natural theology. First, it presumes that humans seek autonomy and self-sufficiency, apart from God's gracious action. In short, it is anthropocentric, while it denies God's freedom to act.

Second, it pieces together ideas 'about God' into an abstraction that is far different from the God of biblical revelation. Because it is anthropocentric it creates, if you will, its own *image* of God. Third, it always takes the shape of the beliefs and values of a particular culture and class of people that develop its implications for doctrine, ethics, and preaching. It domesticates the gospel, which results a in particular kind of secular reductionism. This last issue, of course, demonstrates Barth's linkage of natural theology to the ideology of Nazism. For this discussion see, K. Barth, *Church Dogmatics* II/1, (Edinburgh: T&T Clark, 1957) 84ff.

[57] Originally published as part of the series, *Theologische Existenz Heute* no XXXII. Chr. Kaiser Verlag, 1935. The remaining references to "Gospel and Law" are notified by parentheses.

[58] Eberhard Busch, *The Great Passion: An Introduction to Karl Barth's Theology*. Translated by G. W. Bromiley, (Grand Rapids: Eerdmans, 200) 154.

[59] K. Barth, *Church Dogmatics*, II/2, 511.

[60] In his most developed discussion in *Church Dogmatics* II/2, Barth succinctly states: "The one Word of God is both Gospel *and* Law," K. Barth, *Church Dogmatics* II/2, p. 511ff. He further writes: "As the doctrine of God's command, ethics interprets the law as the form of the gospel, i.e., as the sanctification which comes to man through the electing God," (509).

[61] E. Busch, *Karl Barth: Life and Letters*, 287ff.

[62] J. H. Yoder, *Karl Barth and the Problem of War and Other Essays on Barth*, 182ff.

[63] There is no doubt that Barth was influenced by the Dutch theologian Hendrik Berkhof's 1953 book, *Christ and the Powers*. This book was translated by John Howard Yoder in 1962, and was later published by Herald Press. See Hendrik Berkhof, *Christ and the Powers*, trans. John H. Yoder (Scottdale, Pa.: Herald Press) 1977.

[64] K. Barth, *The Christian Life*. All references to this book will be placed in parentheses in the text.

[65] Regarding these themes, see Clifford Green, (ed.) *Karl Barth: Theologian of Freedom* (London: Collins Publications, 1989); and Timothy Gorringe, *Karl Barth: Against Hegemony*.

[66] Barth's most condensed writing on the "call to discipleship" is found in his *Church Dogmatics,* IV/2 (Edinburgh: T&T Clark, 1958) 533–53. This

text is made more accessible when it was published as K. Barth, *The Call to Discipleship* (Minneapolis: Fortress, 2003).

[67] Although 'Leviathan' is perhaps most obvious in monarchy or dictatorship, Barth argues that any political ideology, once united with the state's power, can destroy the good in human politics. Using the deception that the state stands 'for' its people, as their 'guardian', Leviathan uses any means necessary to "fascinate" and attract its followers, while it "demonizes" its enemies. In separating humanity from God's rule, the state as Leviathan rejects its true identity as the 'outer circle' of the kingdom of God, and in so doing unleashes its havoc in the world.

[68] In *Church Dogmatics* IV/2 Barth dialectically argues that the church is either tempted toward "alienation" (secularization) or the other pole of "self-glorification" (sacralization)," (K. Barth, *Church Dogmatics*, IV/2, 668). The first pole reflects the church that seeks to accommodate itself to the world, and in so doing becomes a 'secular church'. The second is the 'self-glorified' church, which seeks its "self-assertion" in its "particularity of its being and action in the world." It seeks to "represent itself as a world of its own within the world," (669).

[69] K. Barth, *Church Dogmatics*, II/2, 527.

[70] *Ibid.*, 121.

[71] K. Barth, *Church Dogmatics*, IV/3.1, trans. G. Bromiley, (Edinburgh: T&T Clark, 1961) 115. For an excellent discussion of Barth's understanding of 'secular parables of truth', see G. Hunsinger, *How to Read Karl Barth*, pp. 234–80.

[72] Daniel M. Bell, Jr., "State and Civil Society," in Scott and Cavanaugh (eds.), *The Blackwell Companion to Political Theology*, 435.

[73] See John Howard Yoder, *The Priestly Kingdom: Social Ethics as Gospel* (Notre Dame: University of Notre Dame Press, 1984) 135–47.

[74] Yoder repeatedly makes this point in various essays. For these, see John Howard Yoder, *Karl Barth and the Problem of War*, 76–77; 115–18; 141–43; 172–73; and 183–84.

[75] In *Church Dogmatics* IV/2, Barth includes six analogies of church and human law. These include: 1) a grace-driven law of the gospel of servanthood, which transcends the law's tendency to swing between "fulfillment and claim, dignity and responsibility, and taking and giving"; 2) the human subject is not established by political authority or entitlement, thus controlled by the "merry-go-round" of legal validation rhetoric, but

claimed by the grace of Jesus Christ; 3) the church's authority is not based on coercion but trust, which is "the law within the law"; 4) the community is committed to the welfare of all, while rejecting the apparent authority of the powers; 5) every person is an equal regardless of status, capacity, or qualification; 6) church law is "living"—flexible and fluid, "continuously flowing from the worse to the better," Karl Barth, *Church Dogmatics* IV/2, 722ff.

[76] Following Barth's lead, Yoder develops his own five practices of baptism, Eucharist, 'binding and loosing', 'freedom at the meeting', and the 'universality of gifts'. See John Howard Yoder, *Body Politics: Five Practices of the Christian Community Before the Watching World* (Nashville: Discipleship Resources, 1992).

[77] Although dated, George Hunsinger's 1980 essay, "Karl Barth and the Politics of Sectarian Protestantism: A Dialogue with John Howard," succinctly presents two important differences between Yoder and Barth (G. Hunsinger, *Disruptive Grace: Studies in the Theology of Karl Barth* [Grand Rapids: Eerdmans, 2000] 114–28). The first difference is that "Yoder proceeds from the assumption that a predominantly negative relationship underlies any positive connections between the Christian community and the state. Barth's assumption is exactly the reverse, that any negative relationship between the two communities is always undergirded by one that is fundamentally positive," (124). Indeed, continues Hunsinger, "it's only through its relationship to the church that the state makes any positive contribution to the order of redemption." This leads to the second point, that God prioritizes the church over the state in God's divine plan of salvation history. The state and the civil community, as part of unredeemed creation, remain part of the old age that is passing away. In contrast, says Hunsinger, "[for] Barth there is no unredeemed creation," (126).

[78] Karl Barth, *The Christian Life*, 194.

[79] Oliver O'Donovan, *The Desire of the Nations: Rediscovering the Roots of Political Theology* (Cambridge: Cambridge University Press, 1996) 213.

[80] K. Barth, *Church Dogmatics* IV/4 (Edinburgh: T&T Clark, 1969) 146. For a useful discussion on this point, see Biggar, *The Hastening that Waits*, 146–61.

[81] John Milbank, *Theology and Social Theory: Beyond Secular Reason* (Oxford: Basil Blackwell, 1990) 380.

[82] Stanley Hauerwas, *A Community of Character: Toward a Constructive Social Ethic* (Notre Dame: University of Notre Dame Press, 1981) 1.

[83] John Webster, *Word and Church: Essays in Christian Dogmatics*, (Edinburgh: T&T Clark, 2002) 249.

[84] As Nigel Biggar puts it: "Barth never lets us forget that the community is no more absolute than the individual; and that moral character is formed, not simply as the individual is shaped by tradition and custom, but as she responds to the command of God's Word that reaches her through—and often in spite of—her social context." N. Biggar, *Hastening that Waits*, 145.

[85] Jeffrey Stout, *Democracy and Tradition* (Princeton, N.J.: Princeton University Press, 2004) 115.

[86] Ibid., 109. Stout, in his brief discussion of Barth, relies principally on *Church Dogmatics* 4/3.1, and on George Hunsinger's interpretation of Barth's theology in *How to Read Karl Barth: The Shape of His Theology* (New York: Oxford University Press, 1991) and *Disruptive Grace: Studies in the Theology of Karl Barth* (Grand Rapids: Eerdmans, 2000).

[87] The rejection of the world as *alien* usually results in two kinds of Christian action, namely "principle monasticism" and "principle crusadism," in K. Barth, *The Christian Life*, 197ff. The first strategy errors by linking one's personal disdain for the world to a general or systematic strategy of witness for all Christians; it becomes a "principle" instead of an individual perspective. God's freedom to engage individuals *as* individuals in Christian witness is replaced with a principle, an ideological "ism." By privileging the sociality (or ethos) of the church, the personal sphere, including the conscience, becomes reduced to the community, and thus, ironically, "collectivist." The second position stresses the Christian way of life as "superior" to others, and therefore its task or witness is to "teach the world" or "call it to order." Instead of sectarian withdrawal, however, this position leads to a kind of activism, indeed even a militant activism that unites the gospel with particular "intellectual, moral, and even political positions," (198).

GOSPEL AND LAW

I

If I chose the title, *"Law and Gospel,"* I would have to speak in terms of the formula which has come to be taken almost for granted among us. But I should like immediately to call attention to the fact that I shall not speak about "Law and Gospel" but about *"Gospel and Law."* The traditional order, "Law and Gospel," has a perfect right in its place, which we shall later describe. It must not, however, define the structure of the whole teaching to be outlined here. The nature of the case is such that anyone who really and earnestly would first say Law and only then, presupposing this, say Gospel would not, no matter how good his intention, be speaking of the Law of *God* and therefore then certainly not of *his* Gospel. This usual way is, even in the most favorable case, enveloped in ambiguities of every sort.

Anyone who wishes correctly to approach our subject must speak first of the *Gospel.* This makes us think immediately of that 430-year interval after which, according to Galatians 3:17, the Law followed the promise. It *must* follow the promise, but it must *follow* the promise. And while the Law follows the promise, the *fulfillment* of the promise follows it in turn, and this fulfillment, only this, contains the Law's own fulfillment. The Law would not be the Law if it were not hidden and enclosed in the ark of the *covenant.* And the Gospel, too, is only the Gospel if the Law—that which "came in between" (Romans 5:20)—is *hidden* and

71

Law follows promise

Fulfillment of promise follows too & contains Law's fulfillment *enclosed* in it as in the ark of the covenant. The Gospel is not Law, just as the Law is not Gospel; but because the Law is in the Gospel, from the Gospel, and points to the Gospel, we must first of all know about the Gospel in order to know about the Law, and not vice versa.

We must, however, immediately clarify this: anyone who wishes correctly to approach our subject must speak first of the content of the Gospel, of God's grace. We agree on this (how could we justify a different statement in the face of Holy Scripture?): if we speak of Gospel *and* if we speak of Law, we mean God's Word. God's Word can indeed say many things to us. It not only can comfort us, heal us, vivify us, it not only can instruct and enlighten us, it can also judge us, punish us, kill us, and it actually does all of these. But let us not overlook three things:

1. The Word of God is the one "Word of truth," the Word of the "Father of light in whom is no variation or alternation of light and darkness" (James 1:17 f.). According to Scripture, the contrast of Gospel and Law certainly designates a duality. It can even designate a struggle. But their peace in the one Word of this Father is greater than their duality and their struggle.

2. The Word of God, when it is addressed to us and when we are allowed to hear it, demonstrates its unity in that it is always grace; i.e., it is free, non-obligatory, undeserved divine goodness, mercy, and condescension. A Gospel or a Law which we speak to ourselves, by virtue of our own ability and trusting in our own authority and credibility, would, as such, not be *God's* Word; it would not be *his* Gospel and it would not be *his* Law. The *very fact that* God speaks to us, that, under all circumstances, is, in itself, grace.

3. The Word of God preserves this its form by being also in its content, whatever it says, properly and ultimately *grace: free, sovereign* grace, *God's* grace, which therefore can also mean being Law, which also means judgment, death, and hell, but *grace* and nothing else. Every

72

Content of Gospel

Gospel or Law that we speak to ourselves is not God's Word

apparently different content which we could ascribe to the
Word of God proves, considering the Old Testament pre-
dictive witness as well as the New Testament witness of fulfillment, to be included in this as relative to this content,
to God's grace. A word of God with a really different content would as such, in any case, not be a Word of the
triune God, whom Holy Scripture proclaims. If we hear this
Word of God, then we hear—grace. Precisely because the
Gospel has grace as its *particular direct* content, which then
also includes, in itself, the content of the Law, it enforces
its *priority* over the Law which still, included in the Gospel
and relative to it, is no less God's Word.

Thus it is above all necessary that we speak of this content of the Gospel. God's *grace*, which is this content—which
also includes the Law, if it really is *God's* Word and Law
—this grace is called, and is, *Jesus Christ.* For this is God's
grace, that the eternal Word of God *became flesh.* Flesh
means "like one of us." God's Word does not transform himself into flesh. How would it be grace if God ceased to be
God, even if he could? What kind of mercy would he show
us thereby? No, that the Word *became* flesh means that
without ceasing to be God, he added our humanity to and
assimilated it in his deity, in indissoluble but also unmixed
unity with himself; and let us be clear, this refers to our
humanity in the shape resulting from sin's darkening and
destruction. Therefore, this was done not for the sake of
the power or honor or any other attribute of humanity, but
because of the Word's own good pleasure, because of his
incomprehensible love and that which is the sign: "born of
the Virgin Mary." This is God's grace: our ordinary humanity is not the only humanity, but in Jesus Christ, God's own
humanity, the humanity of his Word, and in him, in this
his abasement to our lowliness, his divinity is present for
us others; we participate in his divinity, we are exalted to
him. And now this eternal Word of God, because he bore
flesh, has borne the need, the curse, the punishment which
stamps and characterizes man as flesh. This punishment is

*our ordinary humanity
is not the only humanity*

God's answer to the sin of man. Sin consists in autocracy, but thus to absolutize the self is godlessness. That this is true becomes apparent in man's aversion and flight precisely from the grace of God. God's answer to sin—this is also grace—is our being as flesh: we must die. If we would *hear* this answer, this would be our *salvation*. We would then, considering that we must die (Psalms 90:12), in the knowledge of our lostness as the people that is grass (Isaiah 40:7), repent and, our autocracy destroyed, inherit eternal life. For one reason and one alone does God will the death of the godless: that he turn away from his nature and live (Ezekiel 18:21 f., and parallels). But who hears this answer? Who acknowledges it? Who bows before it? None of us! At this point, God's grace runs into our hatred of grace. But this is the proper work of grace, that his eternal Word —by his becoming flesh, by his remaining obedient in the flesh, by his suffering punishment and therefore dying, because of this obedience—undertook to give the saving answer in our place, to expose our human autocracy and godlessness, to confess man's lostness, to acknowledge the justice of God's judgment against us, and thus to accept the grace of God. This is what Jesus Christ did for us "during his whole lifetime on earth, but especially at its end" (answer to question 37 of the Heidelberg catechism). He quite simply *believed*. (πίστις Ἰησοῦ in Romans 3:22; Galatians 2:16, etc. should certainly be understood as a subjective genitive!) And in this faith, he bore our punishment—not first of all, for instance, to give us an example (he certainly also did that!), but first of all and above all representatively. This is God's grace: that our humanity is, insofar as it is ours, not only condemned and lost because of our sins (our perpetually new sins!) but at the same time, insofar as it is the humanity of Jesus Christ, it is justified by God and accepted *in* the judgment and *in* the lostness because Jesus Christ—only the eternal Word of God could do this —believed; i.e., he said not "no" but "yes" to grace and thus to man's state of being judged and lost. But this justifica-

74

tion and acceptance of our humanity is really accomplished in the *resurrection* of Jesus Christ from the *dead*. God's eternal Word in his unity with the flesh is not only the promise but the fulfillment of the promise that man's repentance will be his salvation, that the just will *live* by his faith. Therefore, because he took the form of a servant and thus and therein was obedient unto death, God has exalted him (Philippians 2:6f.). Grace also triumphed and revealed itself as grace in him, the one and only person who allowed God's grace validity as grace in the flesh, because he was the eternal Word that became flesh. The one who accepted death as the wages of sin—and thus precisely preserved his sinlessness—this is the one whom death could not hold, the one whose life had to *devour* death, and *did*. And this is God's grace, that we can see as the end of all humanity, insofar as it is ours, certainly nothing else ahead of us except the infirmity of old age, the hospital, the battlefield, the cemetery, decay, or ashes; but to the extent that it is at the same time the humanity of Jesus Christ, just as definitely—no, much more definitely—nothing else ahead of us but resurrection and eternal life.

Consequently, God's grace, his grace for our humanity, the goodness, mercy, and condescension in which he is our God and as such accepts us, is Jesus Christ, he himself and he uniquely. He himself and he uniquely is therefore the content of the Gospel. Grace, and that means the content of the Gospel, consists therefore simply in the fact that Jesus Christ with his humanity, which he assumed in his birth, preserved as obedience in his death, glorified in his resurrection—he himself and he uniquely intercedes for us with our humanity. He *can* do it because he is not only like one of us but is God's son and thus himself God, the judge before whom he undertakes the responsibility for us. And he *does* it, because it is his unfathomable pleasure to make this use of his divine power, to utilize a love which expects no love in return and finds none, which encounters us only and always and in all cases as free and pure love. According

Jesus is content of Gospel

to this, the state and course of the *man* under grace must be characterized as the state and course of one for whose humanity Jesus Christ *intercedes* with his assumed, obedient, and glorified humanity and does so because man himself and of himself has neither any willingness nor ability to believe. Jesus Christ intercedes completely so that thus man's own humanity, as Paul likes to put it, is dead, but is alive only because he is "in Christ," i.e., because Jesus Christ has become, grammatically speaking, his subject. "I have been crucified with Christ. I live, but no longer I, but Christ lives in me. For the life I now live in the flesh, I live in the faith of the Son of God" (this is to be understood quite literally: I live—not, for instance, somehow in my belief in the Son of God, but in the fact that the Son of God believed!), "who loved me and gave himself for me" (Galatians 2:20). The state and course of the man under grace is thus expressed in the Old Testament: "He who dwells in the shelter of the Highest, and abides in the shadow of the Almighty, says to the Lord: My refuge and my fortress, my God in whom I hope" (Psalms 91:1). That he is in the communion of the saints, that he has received the forgiveness of sins, that he is hastening toward the resurrection of the body and the life everlasting—these things this man believes, but they have no reality, they have not even a partial reality in his faith, in the triumph of his faith; they only have reality in the fact that the Lord Jesus Christ, who was born a man for us, died for us and rose for us, is also his Lord, his refuge, his fortress, his God. Jesus Christ, he himself and he alone is the grace bestowed upon such a man.

II

Now, in the second place, it is time to speak of the *Law*. We have said that just as the Gospel is not the Law, the Law is not the Gospel. We would contradict the whole of Holy Scripture if we were unwilling to distinguish between the two. But we could also not, according to what we have

76

can't separate the two

said, glance over from the Gospel to the Law as to a second entity next to and outside of the Gospel. We would, again, contradict the whole of Holy Scripture if we wished to separate the two here. If we wish to avoid both mistakes, we must now proceed from what Scripture indubitably attests concerning *Jesus Christ* (of whom we heard: he is grace, he is the content of the Gospel), i.e., that he has satisfied *Jesus satisfied the Law* the Law, has fulfilled the Law, keeping it by obedience to its commands. In defining the Law, we shall in no case be permitted to break loose from this fact—that Jesus Christ, because he was the "evident grace of God" (Titus 2:11), at the same time kept the commands of the Law; instead, we shall have to begin with it. This fact will not only form the criterion by which we must measure all of our self-constructed concepts of Law and norm. It will also have to become the canon of interpretation of everything called Law in the Old Testament and New Testament: the deciding element, that which is really intended in every great or small, internal or external command, has to be understood from the fulfillment of each of them in Jesus Christ.

"The Law is the manifest will of God." The definition is correct. But where is the will of God manifest? Certainly God is the Creator of all things and thus Lord of all that occurs. He and his will, and thus the Law, are, however, not manifest to us in all things, in every occurrence, that is, so very manifest that our apprehensions of it could claim to be more and something different than our own theories and interpretations. If the Law is also *God's Word*, if it is further *grace* that God's Word is spoken aloud and becomes audible, and if grace means nothing else than *Jesus Christ*, then it is not only uncertain and dangerous but perverse to want to understand the Law of God on the basis of any other thing, of any other event which is different from the event in which the will of God, tearing in two the veil of our theories and interpretations, is visible as grace in both form and content. This event is, however, the occurrence of the will of God at Bethlehem, at Capernaum and

Tiberias, in Gethsemane, on Golgotha and in the garden of Joseph of Arimathea. Because this occurrence of the will of God, therefore the occurrence of his grace, becomes *manifest* to us, the *Law* becomes manifest to us. From what God does *for us, we infer what he wants with us and from* us. His grace does apply to *us*, it does concern us. Also, and precisely in his grace, he does demonstrate that he certainly acts for us and toward us, but for and toward *us* as his creatures in the relative but real differentiation of their existence and nature as creatures from his as Creator. His action does not revolve in itself; instead, it has its goal in our action, in the conformity of our action with his own. "You must"—more exactly and correctly, "*You shall*"—"be perfect, as your heavenly father is perfect" (Matthew 5:48). Grace can by no means become manifest to men unless it means this offense, unless it moves in this future tense: "You shall be!" Yes, the revelation of grace as such *is* this offense. Given the validity of this indicative, "that I am not my own but his, my faithful Saviour Jesus Christ's," then precisely this its validity establishes the *Ten Commandments*, together with its exposition in the *Sermon on the Mount*, and its application in the *apostolic instructions*. Grace needs only to become known among us. Whether it be originally in the faith of all the Biblical witnesses, as prophecy and expectation through the prophets, or as recollection and proclamation through the apostles, precisely its publication establishes the *Law*. The divine justification of universally sinful men by the faith of Jesus Christ is attested, according to Romans 3:21, by the *Law* and the *prophets*. The promulgation of the divine *commands* proclaims the grace promised in the covenant between God and Israel. But the significance of the New Testament apostolate, which always looks back on the accomplished fulfillment, is also the summons to the Church, and that means to the *obedience* of faith (Romans 1:5); then, therefore, the rejection of its message is decisively designated as disobedience (Romans 10:21; 11:30; 15:31).

And John the Baptist, as the preacher of *repentance*, stands, quite appropriately in the middle between Moses and Paul, pointing to the present Messiah. "You will be!" "All of you will be!" This, and thus God's Law, is what they all perceived in the revelation of the grace in which they participated—it makes no difference whether it meant future, present, or past to them—and transmitted as their witness to this revelation. But God's Law, an entirely definite, demanding, claiming, will of God also meets those who are in the Church—in the *Church*, concretely in its preaching, in its sacraments, in its confession. How could the Lordship of Jesus Christ be proclaimed, unless the proclamation as such be a demand for *obedience?* How the incarnation except as the command of self-denial? How the cross of Christ, except as the command to *follow after* him and take up one's own cross? How then his resurrection except as under the admonition of the Easter pericope of the ancient Church (I Corinthians 5:7 f.): *"Cleanse out the old leaven* that you may be new dough!"*? Precisely faith in the article concerning the standing and falling of the Church (*articulus stantis et cadentis ecclesiae*), in the message about the justification of the sinner through the reconciliation which took place in the blood of Christ, means *purification, sanctification, renewal,* or it means nothing at all; it is unfaith, false faith, superstition. "And by this we may be sure that we know him, if we keep his commandments. He who says, 'I know him' but disobeys his commandments is a liar, and the truth is not in him" (I John 2:3 f.). Yes, and further, the Church would not be the Church if, in her very existence, but also in her teaching and keeping of the Law of God, its *commands,* its *questions,* its *admonitions,* and its *accusations* would not become visible and apprehensible also for the world, for state and society—even if they do not receive precisely the message concerning the grace of the triune God, expressed in the three articles of faith, the message which uniquely constitutes the task of the Church. The Church would not be the Church if these aspects of the

If grace is manifest, it means demand upon men

Law would not, as such, become the prophetic witness *for* the will of God *against* all of men's sinful presumption, *against* all their lawlessness and unrighteousness. Thus, we can certainly make the general and comprehensive statement that the Law is nothing else than the necessary *form of the Gospel, whose content is grace*. Precisely this content demands this form, the form which calls for its like, the Law's form. If grace is manifest, if it is attested and proclaimed, it means demand and claim upon man. If there is faith in Jesus Christ, the one who is coming or has come, if his name is proclaimed, grace means the office of Moses and Elijah, of Isaiah and Jeremiah, the office of the Baptizer, of Paul, of James. Grace, by becoming the summons to grace, means the Church which dares and must dare to speak with authority.

In this way, then, the *Law is in the Gospel* as the tablets from Sinai were in the ark of the covenant, in such a way that the *Gospel is always in the Law* as that which is manifest, proclaimed, as that which concerns man in the crib and in swaddling clothes of the commands, of the command and order of God. Therefore, Paul quite seriously calls the Law holy and its commands holy, right, and good (Romans 7:12). Therefore, he denies that it is against the promises of God (Galatians 3:21). Therefore, he says that it rather promises us life (Romans 7:10). Therefore, he asserts (in agreement with the familiar words of the Sermon on the Mount in Matthew 5:16 f.) that the proclamation of faith means not the abrogation but the establishment of the Law (Romans 3:21). Therefore, he designates himself—and does so, let it be understood, precisely in his character as the apostle to the Gentiles—as one under the Law of Christ (ἔννομος Χριστοῦ, I Corinthians 9:21). Therefore, he can say in prosaic terms, and not at all hypothetically, that only the doers of the Law will be justified (Romans 2:13). Therefore, the praise of the Law, in the form in which it is peculiar to the message concerning Christ in the Old Testament, by no means ceases in that of the New Testament.

80

And why should it? The distinction between Gospel and Law has been compared with that between heaven and earth, or between day and night. The differentiation between content and form, however, also designates an infinite distinction. But what does this distinction mean? It certainly can *not* mean a distinction between more and less, better and worse, or even the distinction between divine and human or good and evil! The fact that there is an earth under the heavens, that day is day in its alternation with night, that the content of the Gospel also has a form, is not simply one more of God's works, but is precisely the work of God which makes room for the Gospel in our human sphere and room for us men in the sphere of the Gospel. In view of this work of God, how could praise be lacking, how could it ever cease? No, the praise of the Law of God, as it is sung for example in Psalm 119, will not grow old throughout all eternity. Although the Law is not the Gospel, without the Law, we would, in fact, not have the Gospel either.

When we come, however, to answer the question, "What does God in his Law want with us and from us?" we shall, unless we wish to go astray, have to come back again in all strictness to the *content* of the Gospel, to the fact that Jesus Christ has fulfilled the Law and kept all the commands. The Law does bear witness to the grace of God; in this way, it is the form of the Gospel, in this way it is claim and demand, call to repentance and prophecy. In testifying to God's grace, it says to us, "You should"—no, "You shall be!" However, God's grace is Jesus Christ, who intercedes for us with his humanity. He intercedes for us, however, by believing in our place—it took the eternal Word incarnate to do that—and that means by saying "yes" to God's glory and thus to man's misery. By this, his believing, he accomplished once for all what God wants with man and from him: he fulfilled the Law and kept all the commands. All the commands point to, they bear witness to this faith, which *he* alone demonstrated. And, therefore,

81

Commands point to the faith that he alone demonstrated

if the Gospel becomes manifest, this faith of Jesus Christ, which is the heart and star of the Gospel, becomes that form which requires conformity, and therefore the command in all commands, the principle of our cleansing, sanctification, and renewal, the One in all that the Church has to say both to itself and to the world. For if Jesus Christ has done *this* in our place, what then becomes of *us?* Men, beloved brothers, what should *we* do then? This question is laid before us and upon us with the entire dignity and gravity of the divine Law itself—and already before the question, its answer: You shall believe! You, you who have other gods beside me, you who make for yourselves pictures of me, who misuse my name, profane the Sabbath, are disobedient to father and mother, who kill, who commit adultery, who steal, who bear false witness against your neighbor, covet what belongs to him—you shall (and that will be the negation and reversal of everything) believe, *you shall* love and fear God, not in contradicting these your sins, not in struggling against them, but in completely and consistently eradicating them, for even the smallest sin would still be the whole, the deadly sin. And this will be your conformity with that form of the Gospel, your obedience, then, to God's law! It is true, therefore, that all commandments are included in the *first* commandment and always must be understood and explained as especially emphasizing the first commandment.

What then does precisely this first commandment mean, if we are not permitted to understand it as anything else than as the form of the Gospel? What does it mean to fear and to love God? What does it mean to believe? The faith of Jesus Christ, in which grace has occurred and at the same time the Law has been fulfilled, is a unique act which cannot be repeated. Once more, this occurrence required the eternal Word in flesh. Being certain Jesus Christ is God but we are men, we will do well not to try to imitate Jesus in this faith and thus to believe *as* Jesus believed. However, the meaning of the first commandment and thus of all the commandments, and thus of our obedience to God's Law, can and must be that we believe *in* Jesus Christ, that we—since the Word became flesh, remained obedient in the flesh, and was exalted in the flesh—acknowledge his representative faith, which we will never realize, and allow it to count as our life, which we do not have here in our hand and at our disposal but have above, hidden with him in God (Colossians 3:1 f.). If grace, the content of the Gospel, concerns us, if it is manifest and thus assumes the form of the Law, it means that we "seek the things which are above" in this quite precise sense. "The Law is spiritual" (Romans 7:14), but that means its sense and its meaning are our life's "being raised with Christ." This is what God wanted of Israel with the first as well as the second table of the Law, with the sacrifice, food and purity commandments, with the constitution as a national-church or ecclesiastical-nation, which he gave Israel as "the shadow of things to come." This is what Jesus wanted of his disciples when he commanded them: "Love your enemies! Be careful how you give alms! Do not be anxious! Do not judge!" This is what the apostles wanted from their congregations when they admonished them to love, to unity, to purity, daily to put aside the old man. This alone can also be the meaning and content of the authority with which the Church confronts its members and the world. We are always concerned with faith in Jesus Christ, who is crucified and risen. Thus there can never be claims and demands which would have legal validity from another source or in themselves: there can only be *witnesses*. And these witnesses will always be concerned with the grace of God, which has accomplished everything for us and whose end must be this accomplishment. By saying *this*, these witnesses *admonish, warn, command, order,* and *prohibit*. They will have legal authority, because and to the extent that they proclaim the "Law of Christ" (Galatians 6:2) and thus the "Law of faith" (Romans 3:21), and thus the "Law of the Spirit of life" (Romans 8:2). And we will keep and fulfill the Law and all its commandments if we have faith in Jesus Christ; that means the faith which clings to him and remains true to him, simply because he is the eternal incarnate Word, which has accomplished all things. This faith includes all obedience. Our works, great and small, internal and external, are accepted if they take place as works of this faith—and they are rejected if they do not. We must provisionally stop at this point, for precisely this faith, which allows Jesus Christ the right to be its representative, is the work and gift of the Holy Spirit, which we cannot appropriate to ourselves, but for which we can only pray.

III

We have spoken in the foregoing of the *truth* of the Gospel and the Law in their mutual relation. On this basis only can we gain insight into their reality, of which we must now speak.

Now we must consider what it means that the Gospel as well as the Law—or, in our previous terms, the content and form of the Gospel—have been put into *our* hands, into the hands of *sinners.*

put into our hands

By becoming manifest, God's grace (and thus the Law) irrefutably and unambiguously illuminates the fact and meaning of our sinfulness. We can measure the *depth* of our sins by the fact that nothing less than God's eternal Word accepted us in this depth and had to do so in such a way that he took our place, pointing us solely to faith, faith in him who is the work and gift of the Holy Spirit! This action also discloses the *nature* of sin, against which God contends in Jesus Christ, the forgiveness of which he has prepared for us in him. If this forgiveness is based on God's doing in our place, for us, what is right in his sight, then our sin consists in our very inability to appear for ourselves, but still *wishing* to do so. As we have already said, sin consists in autocracy and in godlessness, inasmuch as God is

84

essentially gracious; but precisely our autocracy attests and means our rejection of grace and our self-assertion against God, our separation from God.

By accepting us in the gift of the Gospel and the Law, God lays this gift in our hands, in the presumptuous hands of those who, contrary to the significance and definition of this gift, desperately wish to appear on our own behalf, because we wish to assert ourselves. What will we start thereby, we who wish by all means to "start something" with everything and everyone? Notice carefully, God lays his gift in our hands *nevertheless* and, in spite of the worse than questionable purity of our hands, it is and remains *his* gift. The fourth section of this lecture discusses the *positive* meaning of this "nevertheless." But first of all, it means something *negative*. And this negative entity forms the background against which the positive one must stand out in order to be recognized as such. Thus we must speak first of the negative.

The nature of the matter requires that we turn above all now to our dealings with the *Law* of God. God's grace, by coming to us, does have the form of Law, of commandment, of requirement, of claim. What will happen if we, we sinners, perceive this claim? Paul, especially in Romans 5 and 7, gave the fundamental answer: our sin uses the Law as a springboard (ἀφορμή Romans 7:8, 11) and celebrates its resurrection (Romans 7:8 f.), becomes active and recognizable (Romans 7:7) as "sin which dwells within us" (Romans 7:20), as sinful "Law in our members" (Romans 7:23), only by winning control (Romans 5:20), by becoming "sinful beyond measure" (Romans 7:13), by producing—through misusing the Law itself—its master stroke, so to speak, distorting precisely the good, precisely the best, into its opposite (Romans 7:13), using it to deceive (Romans 7:11). Compared with it, what is the sin of the man whom the Law of God has *not* encountered? Paul, as Romans 1:18 f. shows, really took this latter sin seriously, and yet he had to call it downright "dead" (Romans 7:8) next to the sin of which the man who encounters God's law is guilty. Only in this sin is the nature of sin visible and understandable. But what is this gigantic deception which sin perpetrates by means of the Law? Paul answers: it consists in the fact that sin causes covetousness to shoot up in us, precisely in the face of the Law's "Thou shalt not covet." We must not allow ourselves to be misled to interpret this "lust" moralistically because of associations which arise in connection with the analogy of the classical *nitimur in vetitum*. . . . What we moralistically define as "lust," especially sexual libido to which the Church's exposition seems to have turned all too rapidly and all too zealously, certainly is, so Paul thinks, one of the consequences of that sin which is indeed to be taken seriously but, in comparison to what concerns us here, is "dead." The Law of which Paul speaks is indeed *spiritual*, and so, in the case of the deception which sin perpetrates by awakening that lust for what is forbidden, just as in the deception of the snake in the story of the first fall, it must be a deception relating precisely to the *spiritual* character of the Law. We derive its definition from a different passage in which Paul speaks concretely of the person deceived through sin's use of the Law. He says of the Jews who have crucified Christ and rejected him right up to the present: "They have a zeal for God, but it is unenlightened. For, being ignorant of the justification that comes from God, and seeking to establish their own, they did not submit to justification by God. For Christ is the end of the Law, for justification" (Romans 10:2 f.). This then is the lust which causes sin to shoot up within us because of the Law—precisely the lust of that scribe, who asked, "What must I do to inherit eternal life?" and whom Jesus simply reminded of the Law, of whom it is finally said, "But he desired to justify himself" (Luke 10:29). As a matter of fact, who at that time desired anything else if God's claim encountered him? This lust is human disobedience discovered at its root! For what happens when one confronted with God's claim endeavors to establish his own

86

GOSPEL AND LAW

righteousness? Apparently he makes out of God's claim a
claim of his own, namely the claim that he can and will
himself satisfy God's demands. Why is this disobedience?
It is disobedience because God's claim bears witness to what
is promised to us and fulfilled in Christ, our justification
through this very Christ. *Christ* is indeed the goal of the
Law and is so for our justification. It would be obedience
for us to subordinate ourselves to this justification, to live a
life in this subordination. But our lust shoots right past this
very thing. Why? We do not recognize that the Law proclaims our justification by God. "To this day, whenever
Moses is read, a veil lies over their minds" (II Corinthians
3:15). Why is this true? Why do we not know what we
could still read in the Law? Precisely this is sin's deception,
because we are, from the very start, engaged in asserting
ourselves and advocating our cause, we conceal from ourselves the greatest thing, the decisive element in the Law,
the content of which it is only the form, the healing and
sanctifying grace, in order to strengthen, confirm, exalt ourselves, to represent ourselves as worthy co-workers of God,
meanwhile concerned, with the help of its "letters" because
they are, after all, divine letters, to observe them all and to
do them justice to the best of our knowledge and in good
conscience. Completely occupied with ourselves, we have
made the divine "You shall be!" of the Law into the human
—all too human—"You ought!" This is what Paul called the
"weakening of the Law by the flesh" (Romans 8:3). To
quote his converse formulation, the Law is the *power* of sin
(I Corinthians 15:56). From hence, on the basis of this deception of sin, comes the "unenlightenment" of our "zeal
for God." Just let no one think that, because it is based on
ignorance and because it always is a zeal for *God*, it is a
relatively harmless and forgivable zeal, perhaps to be regretted on account of its imperfection but nevertheless to be
praised on account of its good intention. No, its ignorance
is *disobedience*, and it is a *lie* to call it zeal for God! *Sin*
triumphs in this zeal, more, infinitely more, than in what

87

we think we know as idolatry, blasphemy, murder, adultery, and robbery; infinitely more because here, in his gift of the Law, in the misinterpreted decalogue, in the misinterpreted prophetic utterances, in the misinterpreted Solomonic wisdom, in the misinterpreted Sermon on the Mount and apostolic admonition, God himself has been made the cause and pretext of sin. Now man certainly does pounce, one on this, another on that letter and shred of the Law, with the entire passion of his caprice, victorious and left to itself by God, and at the same time with the entire passion of his bad conscience and surely, absolutely surely, taking the line of least resistance. Each pounces on that portion which he thinks he can best use and each with the triumphant thought that he, with his letter and shred in hand, sooner or later brings about—at least in the eyes of men—a kind of special justification of his own existence. Here is one in a blind frenzy of work; there is one leading an exemplary life as citizen and family man. Here is one in pursuit of "interesting" views, experiences, acquaintances, connections; there is one living with a demonstrative simplicity and frugality. Here is one engaged in the sovereign vagaries of a gypsying genius. Here is one sunk in a wrangling ecclesiastical orthodoxy and theological pedantry; there is one living in perpetually smiling evangelical freedom. Here is one involved in a busy, philanthropic, or, still better, a pedagogical welfare enterprise for all sorts of "lame ducks" among his fellow men; there is one immersed in an undertaking of far-reaching vision for world improvement on a large scale. Here is one living in the solemn whim of a private existence patterned after absolutely nothing else than his own highly individual conception; there is one living in a justice in step with the great mass and the temper of the times, and one living precisely against it, in a refined way. And here is one imbued with the fantastic plan of attempting to live for once with absolute honesty, with absolute purity, with absolute selflessness, with absolute love. Vanity of vanities! What next? In what direction can one not plunge if he once ignores and bypasses the faith which God in Jesus Christ demands for himself and himself alone? There are then a thousand works of the Law, the Law torn into a thousand shreds, a thousand servitudes to which we subject ourselves, a thousand letters on each of which some little man or even many at the same time can cling in order to sip their own righteousness from it. We poor tipplers— always sipping and yet always thirsting again! A harmless, an even partly praiseworthy lust? No, for precisely this lust produces, in visible and invisible extensions of this our "good" efforts, that which, this time, not men but God, in his Law, calls idolatry, blasphemy, murder, adultery, and robbery (see Romans 2:12 f.). This our lust, this our zeal— is it for God? No, with the help and to the honor of God, it is for our own godlessness—which crucified Christ and crucifies him again and again in the midst of Christendom (Hebrews 6:6). Does this still not say enough about what it means for God to give his Law into our hands?

In order to understand what happens to the Law in this case—it is and does remain God's Law!—we must now ask the question, "What happens to the *Gospel*, which is the sense and content of the Law?" It, naturally, does not mean, for instance, that the Gospel would be completely discarded and forgotten if sin deceive us with the Law and therefore about the Law. Sin triumphs even with respect to the Law only in its misuse, not, however (for good reason, not), in its abandonment! And, on the other hand, that deception cannot mean that though the Law be misused, desecrated, corrupted, the Gospel would be preserved intact and thus that we would understand grace as grace after, as well as before. No, the content falls and is corrupted with the form, the Gospel also falls with God's Law. Of the people of Israel, which did not listen to Moses and especially to the first commandment of the Law proclaimed through Moses, which rejected and stoned its prophets, which finally crucified its Messiah, of this people, Isaiah said that they talk of nothing but "covenant" (Isaiah 8:12);

89

Jews, in their failure, still focused on "covenant"

they have always known *much* and thought *highly* of God's grace, patience, and forgiveness of sins—and this is most true precisely on the day of Golgotha. The Pharisees were *far* from being as Pharisaic as we, for the sake of simplicity, imagine them. Did not they, too, wish to escape the coming wrath (Matthew 3:7)? Were not they, too, interested enough to invite Jesus to eat with them? One short and unessential step beyond them we bump into a Christianity which, with respect to the Law, has likewise fallen prey to sin's deception and thus, wishing to justify itself, no longer thinks at all about keeping that which is greatest and most decisive in the Law; nevertheless, it, too, does not ignore the Law; it, too, would like to use grace and harness grace as a counterpoise to temper its unwise zeal for God. But what does grace mean in this case? Here Jesus Christ, who gives everything to his own by himself appearing with God's majesty in their place, has become a demigod, who imparts pretended powers to them, a sort of magic talent, the presence of which can be established like that of any other talent, which they are free to control and direct as their possession, which redounds to their honor before themselves and before others, in which they believe they have a good support for their efforts to assert, to advocate, to justify themselves, with which they intend to comfort themselves (secretly, this is the most important of all), in case as a result of the incompleteness of their efforts there should be disappointments and standstills and, here and there, even simply failure. Jesus Christ becomes the indispensable companion, the useful lever arm, and finally and above all the stopgap for all our efforts toward our own justification! Jesus Christ becomes the personification of the wonderful ideas which we always invent for the sake of this justification, according to whatever the spirit and taste of our time may be! Jesus Christ becomes the great creditor who again and again is just good enough to cover the cost of our own ventures in righteousness! This is what becomes of grace, of the Gospel. In the shadow of sin's deception with the

resisting true grace, the biggest problem

Law, *this* must inevitably happen to the Gospel. There grace is discarded, there Christ has died in vain (Galatians 2:21), for there the offense, the saving offense of the cross, has been removed (Galatians 5:11). There we find sheer enmity against the cross (Philippians 3:18). This is the way Paul spoke of the Christianity which thrives in the shadow of this deception. It is certain that the Gospel, deformed and distorted in this way, cannot mean "the power of God for salvation" (Romans 1:16), if the deformed and distorted Law should, for instance, lead us into the temptation of which we have yet to speak. *This* Jesus Christ has not yet even helped or comforted, much less saved a single man in the temptation which must necessarily follow sin's deception.

And now we can answer the question: "If our autocracy takes possession of it, what then becomes of the Law of God under that deception of sin?"

At this point, we only touch upon the fact that in this deformation and distortion the Law is exposed to every falsification: now—that is, if we are dealing with our pretended obedience to the Law for our self-justification—natural law, or an abstract "reason," or history, or, in these recent troubled times, the "Volksnomoi" (people's laws), so happily invented, may undertake to give to the Law of God the content usable and desirable for this purpose. We only touch upon the fact that its interpretation now, if Christ is not to be its goal, will vacillate unsteadily between a *nomianism* which believes it should submit to these or those observances and disciplines, and an *antinomianism* of pure inwardness, averse to every concrete command and tie. Both nomianism and antinomianism are, of course, forms of "righteousness by works," and we only touch upon the fact, brought out by Paul in Galatians 4:8 f., that the service of the Law, robbed of promise and thereby dishonored and emptied—in plain language but in the most concrete seriousness—represents the relapse out of belief in the one living God into the impoverished *heathen worship of the elements.*

91

not really belief in God

If God be not still God in his Law, then it and he have become only too similar to many other laws and many other gods which do also exist, and it will then become an enticing game to interchange him and his law with these others. Anyone who has once allowed himself to take his life in his own hand in this or that form of "righteousness by works" should, if he is wise enough, just be sure not to forget the eternal, brazen, great laws of his fate, his cosmic-sidereal antagonist, he just should not leave the calendar of his astrological possibilities for this week and for next autumn too far out of reach. It is also typical of a life under the Law which has been dishonored and emptied by our autocracy that we, like bad boys waiting for the teacher, must peer around in interstellar space, keeping a lookout for something which perhaps would still come over us and what it might mean for us. It is also typical of this our life that that calendar is really much more interesting to us than the Bible!

All of that is terrible enough, but it is still only a symptom of the much more terrible judgment which is based on the fact that *God will not be mocked* even in his dishonored and empty Law, that it remains God's claim on men, even if man subjects it to his own claims. What if God still wants his law to be fulfilled, his commandments kept? Yes, how could he fail to stand firm, how could he, as certainly as he is God, retreat from this? And what if God now takes us at our word, holds us to our bold plan and program of fulfilling his Law ourselves and in this, our fulfilling of the Law, to be our own advocates? How would it be if he would really require us to keep the smallest of his commandments even halfway, or even to a small degree? But no, God doubtless demands a total keeping of all his commandments. Now, *justify* yourself if you have been *condemned* precisely from the start and basically by thinking you can and should justify yourself! ! We can "have an unenlightened zeal for God" throughout our lives—and no doubt we all do just that!—but behind this stands the immovable fact (in the whole immovability of the grace of God which is apparent

92

"we refuse him faith in order to believe in ourselves"

in his Law) that God will not be deceived, that we as a whole and singly are discovered to be those who refuse him faith in order to be able to believe in ourselves and trust ourselves that much better. Behind all this stands the fact that this means judgment on all our works by which we think we can justify ourselves, and above all on the works of our faith by which we think we can justify ourselves. For if any one of our works were to be judged as sin against the first commandment, then it certainly would be the one we consider our best, the work of our faith in the Arian and Pelagian Christ, on whom we bestow the honor of just allowing him to remain the innocent useful periphery of our self-assertion. If this is the case with our best work, what about all the others? The horrible thing, which now—corresponding to sin's deception—becomes a reality between God and man, has often been described. At this point, I only mention the result: we have actually refused justification by God. Our self-justification has not succeeded because it is an impossibility. Thus we have no—no justification. I certainly can will—yes, in fact, only too well—but I cannot accomplish the good. How could I, since my very willing is, as that of a deceived deceiver, corrupt? This is what the Law, the Law we have dishonored and emptied, which still is and remains God's Law, has to say to us now. Temptation is present if we must awake from the intoxication of our lust, which shot up by virtue of sin in view of the Law, and must see that nothing has changed about the Law and its demands, if we hear again the real Law and if we now can perhaps no longer hear anything else than the real Law of God, which has *this* to say to us: you certainly can will but you cannot accomplish the good! Not only your sins, no, your good works are sinful, because, perhaps to a greater extent than those things you consider your sins, they are works of your lust *against* God!—in this moment, temptation is present. Now we only know about God's revelation that he is rightly angry with us, that to a thousand words we have not one to answer him, that we thus are lost, have

good works are most against God

fallen prey to death and hell. And what should now happen to us, since when we forfeited the Law, we forfeited also and precisely grace? This is what happens to the Law of God in our hands—it is now the "Law of sin and death" (Romans 8:2), the executor of divine wrath (Romans 4:15), the Law which Paul—not invariably but as a rule—calls the "Nomos," against service to which, against the works of which, against the righteousness of which, and against the servitude and curse of which he can only warn his congregations most urgently. This is the Law, the "office" of which he says in II Corinthians 3:2 f. is to "preach condemnation," even to "kill by the letter." This is the Law which was later so gravely mentioned in the same breath with the whore, reason, with sin and death, in fact with the devil, so urgently depicted as *the* enemy of faith, love, and hope, as *the* great antagonist of the Gospel. This is the Law of which it was said and must be said: either entirely the Law and then death, or entirely the Gospel and then life, there is no third possibility. It is the Law, dishonored and emptied by sin's deception, which, with the power of the *wrath* of God, nevertheless is and remains *his* Law. If we serve *this* Law, then there is no escape from God's judgment, and in the temptation in which this judgment is manifest, there is no counsel, no comfort, no help.

This is the negative entity which follows from the fact that God lays his gift in our hands nevertheless, in spite of our being sinners. This is *one* side of the reality of the mutual relationship of the Gospel and the Law. The Epistle to the Galatians speaks of this negative element—to be sure, not just of it, but quite emphatically also of it.

IV

We announce the *positive* element, which now and only now must be stated in view of this "nevertheless," in the words of the same Paul: "The Law intervened, so that the trespass became stronger; but where sin became stronger,

94

precisely there grace overflowed, so that as sin reigned in death, now grace reigns through justification to eternal life through Jesus Christ our Lord" (Romans 5:20 f.). For "God has consigned all men to disobedience, that he may have mercy upon all. O the depth of the riches both of the wisdom and the knowledge of God! How unsearchable are his judgments and how inscrutable are his ways! 'For who has known the mind of the Lord, or who has been his counsellor?' 'Or who has given a gift to him that he might be repaid?' For from *him* and through *him* and to *him* are all things. To *him* be glory forever. Amen" (Romans 11:32 ff.). Yes, it is unsearchable and inscrutable—it belongs to another order than that of action and reaction, merit and worthiness, it has its beginning and its end only in him —that God does lay his gift, his Word, the Gospel, and the Law in our sinful, impure hands and now that which must happen does happen: just now and only now do we rebel, we corrupt and disgrace precisely his Word, just now and now more than ever, Jesus Christ is crucified with the help and to the honor of God. But, just as the *Law* is and remains the Law of God even though dishonored and emptied by our lust, so—no, not so but still much more, God's *Gospel* is laid precisely in our sinful, unclean hands and after everything has worked itself out, just at this point, the Gospel also operates fully for the first time, it also shows itself fully for the first time for what it is, the really *glad* tidings for *real* sinners.

But is not then our real sin that we, "pursuing justification through the Law" (Romans 9:31), do not hear the Gospel in the Law, do not wish to allow Christ to be the end of the Law? What kind of power can one expect grace to have if we scorned and despised, even hated it? To this, we must answer: God is God. Power, the power of the resurrection (Philippians 3:10) belongs, in any case, precisely and in the first place to grace, which we scorned and despised, even hated; belongs to the Christ, who to this very day has been delivered into the hands of sinners, crucified, dead and buried. "Behold, I make all things new!" Before this "I" no flesh, really none, should be able to boast, not even of its non-resistance! Its regeneration begins precisely at that point at which, as far as we are concerned, absolutely nothing else is real than that we compromise ourselves before him and for him, that point at which the phrase, "I do *not* nullify the grace of God" (Galatians 2:21) can only pass our lips as the acknowledgment of a gift and a miracle which happens to us, and with the acknowledgment, "I am the most distinguished of sinners" (I Timothy 1:15). Precisely and only for this most distinguished sin in all of us, for the sin which became inordinately sinful as the sin against his very person, Jesus became a man, died, and rose again. And thus the victory of the Gospel, the victory of grace is precisely God's victory over this *real* sin, over the sin of our misuse of the *Law*, the sin of our *unbelief.*

We shall have to consider this unsearchable, this inscrutable victory, this victory whose honor is the honor of God, from three points of view:

In the first place, the grace of God, Jesus Christ himself, converts precisely the *judgment*, under which the misused and yet valid law of God places us, into our *justification*. He reveals himself as the Saviour through the Law also in this shape. He vivifies through the Gospel in which he kills through the Law. Now this order, "Law and Gospel," becomes legitimate and meaningful! Through the *content* of the Gospel, thus through himself, he awakens, to the life of faith in him as the one who justifies us, our very existence, which was, through the form of the Gospel, through the Law, condemned and expelled into hell because of our unbelief, our existence as it is in all its nakedness and ugliness, thus including our unbelief. This is true in spite of the fact that we are sinners from head to toe, in our heart and in our deeds—no, precisely because we stand before him thus and only thus! We must emphasize that free grace, Jesus Christ himself, does that. We could not do it ourselves, as

96

"He vivifies through the Gospel in which He kills through the Law" certainly as we do not have in us what it takes, and as certainly as we are still much less able to bestow it on ourselves from outside ourselves. Our justification in the judgment also does not, however, occur on the strength of an immanent lawfulness, as that by which night and day, winter and spring, pain and joy, anxiety and rest follow each other, or in the prudence of the function of a mechanism once arranged in a definite way, or according to the rule of that Absolute Spirit which through Thesis and Antithesis finally returns to itself. The order Law-Gospel, sin-righteousness, which here concerns us is characterized by its identity with the order death-life. But that means it is entirely unintelligible to us as an order. It can only be event and *fact* and we can of ourselves believe it only as the promise of what Jesus Christ does for us, and our belief will be a source of amazement to us. We shall only *really* be able to believe, without knowing whether what we are thus doing is possible. And if Jesus Christ becomes manifest to us through the Law which judges us, if the Law thus becomes the disciplinarian preparing us for him (Galatians 3:24), if we, who amaze ourselves, believe *in him* in our unbelief and despite our unbelief, then this our faith certainly contains in it the decisive knowledge of our sin and the certainty of its forgiveness; but as our faith can now, as faith, only wish to be faith *in him,* as it lives and has its being entirely in him as its object and in no sense in itself, so also our awareness of sin and certainty of forgiveness, and thus our certainty of salvation, become absolutely nothing else than knowledge and certainty *coming from him,* and cannot in any sense be a knowledge and certainty based on themselves and thus knowledge and certainty resulting in any sort of praise for us. The victorious Gospel is the power of God for salvation to everyone who has faith (Romans 1:16). Thus and only thus is it the really *victorious* Gospel despite our sinful, unclean hands.

In the second place, the grace of God, Jesus Christ himself, makes us free from that "Law of sin and death" (Ro-

97

free from Law of sin
and death

mans 8:2). If we are, as the victorious Gospel tells us, justified in him, without ourselves and against ourselves, against
our disobedience and unbelief, then that still means that
this Law cannot condemn us on account of our disobedience and unbelief. Even as "the Law of sin and death," it
has the right and power to condemn us only because it is
God's Law. But if God is for us, has confined us in unbelief in order to have mercy upon us, just this way, precisely in the form of an awakening of the dead, who can
be against us? Certainly not the right and power of his own
Law! Our double anxiety before the Law is now thus also
cast into that confinement of our unbelief: both the anxiety
before its letters, whether or not we know them all and
whether or not we intend to do them justice, and the anxiety
before the consequences of the fact that we certainly are
disobedient to the whole of it because we do not believe—
taken together, the two parts of this double anxiety make
up our fear of life. *It shall no longer be!* God's mercy bends
over that confinement into which this anxiety is cast and
that means that this anxiety can now only be one overcome,
comforted, set at rest, surrounded by a solid shore of hope
and joy. But this liberation reaches deeper: if God's Law
does not really condemn us, then it *is* by no means any
longer the "Law of sin and death"! If the Gospel triumphs,
it not only re-establishes itself as overflowing grace, overflowing precisely on its enemies—no, then the *Law*, the
form of the Gospel also is re-established out of the letters to
the totality of its words, of its one single Word, out of the
demand, "You ought!" to the promise, "You shall be!", out
of the claim on our accomplishment to the claim on our
trust. Then the Law no longer speaks as the instrument of
sin's deception and as the organ of God's wrath, but in its
proper original sense as witness, as the revelation of him
who does all things well and asks nothing from us except
that we believe he *will* do all things well. Because the victory of the Gospel also means that, we read expressly in
Romans 7–8 that we have been set free in Christ Jesus

Law is no longer instrument
of sin's deception or organ of
God's wrath

98

"through the Law of the Spirit of life." Let us note well, all that in Christ Jesus! In our liberation, we honor the glory of *his* work. In order to see our liberation, we can only gaze on *him*. In order to be thankful for it, we can only wish to praise *him*. In order to enjoy it, we can only depend on *him*. Aside from him and without him, apart from the mercy of God which he himself is, which bends over us, we remain confined in disobedience, deceived deceivers, in condemnation and the shadow of death afterward just as before. *He* is our freedom. *He* is the victorious Gospel also in this respect, but he *is* it.

In the third place, the grace of God, Jesus Christ himself, gives us what we need so that our justification and liberation which have been accomplished in him may also be a reality in us: the Holy Spirit of power, of love and self-control (II Timothy 1:7). It gives us the Spirit of *power* to depend on him in an ultimately imperturbable clarity and truth, to depend on him and to remain in him, although, no, precisely because, we must recognize that we are entirely incapable of that. It gives us the Spirit of *love* for him who is the fulfillment of the Law (Romans 13:10) because love allows us, together with all his people bearing each other's burden (Galatians 6:2) and thus also united with him, to gaze on his revealed will, as the bride gazes at the bridegroom, although, no, precisely because, of ourselves we love neither him nor our neighbor. It gives us, finally, the Spirit of *self-control*, which shall always preserve us from forgetting this "although" and "because," from forgetting that, after as before, we ourselves want, to our own ruin, to be like God, knowing good and evil, the self-control which will drive us thus again and again to look and listen to him as our Saviour. This gift of the Holy Spirit is no magic, no enchantment. Anyone who can interpret it thus does not know it. It is, quite wonderfully but also quite soberly, our transfer to the place and status of those in whose defeat the victory of the Gospel, and thereby our justification and thereby the revelation of the Law as

99

the "Law of the Spirit of life," has become real. One will always recognize those who have the Holy Spirit by the fact that they recognize themselves as those who are *poor* before God. These who are, in this sense, poor in spirit (Matthew 5:3) are those in whose sinful, unclean hands the Gospel and the Law have been laid, not in vain but for their salvation, because, through the body of Christ crucified for us and his blood shed for us, they are fed and satisfied and sustained unto eternal life.

CHURCH AND STATE

The title "Justification and Justice"* indicates the question with which I am dealing in this work.

First of all, I will state the question thus: is there a connection between justification of the sinner through faith alone, completed once for all by God through Jesus Christ, and the problem of justice, the problem of human law? Is there an inward and vital connection by means of which in any sense human justice (or law), as well as divine justification, becomes a concern of Christian faith and Christian responsibility, and therefore also a matter which concerns the Christian Church? But we may clearly ask the same question with reference to other conceptions; take the problem of *order*, for instance, of that order which is no longer, or not yet, the order of the Kingdom of God; or the problem of *peace*, which is no longer, or not yet, the eternal Peace of God; or the problem of *freedom*, which is no longer, or not yet, the freedom of the Children of God—do all these problems belong to the realm of the "new creation" of man through the Word of God, do they all belong to his sanctification through the Spirit? Is there, in spite of all differences, an inner and vital connection between the service of God in Christian living indicated in James 1:27 and what we are accustomed to call "Divine Service" in the worship of the Church as such, and another form of service,

* The German title is *Rechtfertigung und Recht.*—ED.

what may be described as a "political" service of God, a service of God which, in general terms, would consist in the careful examination of all those problems which are raised by the existence of human justice, of law, or, rather, which would consist in the recognition, support, defence, and extension of this law—and all this, not in spite of but because of divine justification? In what sense can we, may we, and must we follow Zwingli, who, in order to distinguish them and yet to unite them, speaks in the same breath of "divine and human justice"?

It should be noted that the interest in this question begins where the interest in the Reformation confessional writings and Reformation theology as a whole ceases, or rather, to put it more exactly, where it begins to fade.[1] The fact that both realities exist: divine justification and human justice, the proclamation of Jesus Christ, faith in Him and the office and authority of the secular power, the mission of the Church and the mission of the State, the hidden life of the Christian in God and also his duty as a citizen—all this has been clearly and powerfully emphasized for us by the Reformers. And they also took great pains to make it clear that the two are not in conflict, but that they can very well exist side by side, each being competent in its own sphere. But it must be strongly emphasized that on this point they do not by any means tell us all that we might have expected—not excepting Luther in his work *Of Worldly Authority* of 1523 or Calvin in the majestic closing chapters of his *Institutio*. Clearly we need to know not only that the two are not in conflict, but, first and foremost, to what extent they are connected. To this question, the question as to the relationship between that which they maintained *here* (with the greatest polemical emphasis), and the *centre* of their Christian message, we receive from the Reformers either no answer at all, or, at the best, a very inadequate

[1] Cf. the instructive composition of H. Obendiek: *Die Obrigkeit nach dem Bekenntnis der reformierten Kirche*, Munich, 1936.

answer. Whatever our attitude may be to the content of that last chapter of the *Institutio*, *"De Politica Administratione"* (and, so far as we are concerned, we are prepared to take a very positive position), this at least is clear, that as we look back on the earlier parts of the work, and in particular on the second and third books and their cardinal statements about Jesus Christ, the Holy Spirit, sin and grace, faith and repentance, we feel like a traveller, suddenly transported to a distant land, who is looking back at the country from which he started. For on the question of how far the *politica administratio* in the title of the fourth book belongs to the *externis mediis vel adminiculis quibus Deus in Christi societatem nos invitat et in ea retinet* we shall find only the most scattered instruction, for all the richness which the book otherwise contains. But the same is true of the corresponding theses of Luther and Zwingli, and of those of the Lutheran and Reformed Confessional writings. That authority and law rest on a particular *ordinatio* of divine providence, necessary on account of unconquered sin, serving to protect humanity from the most concrete expressions and consequences of that sin, and thus to be accepted by humanity with gratitude and honour—these are certainly true and biblical thoughts, but they are not enough to make clear the relationship between this issue and the other, which the Reformation held to be the decisive and final issue of faith and confession. What does Calvin mean when, on the one hand, he assures us: *"spirituale Christi regnum et civilem ordinationem res esse plurimum sepositas"*[2]—and on the other hand twice[3] points to the subjection of all earthly rulers to *Christ*, indicated in the passage, Psalms 2:10 ff., and describes the ideal outcome of that divine *ordinatio* as the *politia Christiana?*[4] How far *Christiana?* What has Christ to do with this matter? we ask, and we are left without any real answer, as

[2] *Inst.* IV., 20, 1.
[3] *Ibid.*, 20, 5, and 29.
[4] *Ibid.*, 20, 14.

though a particular ruling of a general, somewhat anonymous Providence were here the last word. And if we read Zwingli's strong statement,[5] that the secular power has "strength and assurance from the teaching and action of Christ," the disappointing explanation of this statement consists only in the fact that in Matthew 22:21 Christ ordained that we should render unto Caesar the things which are Caesar's and unto God the things which are God's, and that by paying the customary "tribute money" (*Didrachmon:* Matthew 17:24 f.) he himself confirmed this teaching. That is again quite true in itself,[6] but, when stated thus apart from its context, in spite of the appeal to the text of the Gospel, it is based not on the Gospel but on the Law.

We can neither overlook nor take lightly this gap in the teaching that we have received from the fathers of our church—the lack of a gospel foundation, that is to say, in the strictest sense, of a Christological foundation, for this part of their creed. There is, of course, no question that here, too, they wished to expound only the teaching of the Bible. But the question remains: in introducing these biblical data into their creed, were they regulating their teaching by the standard which elsewhere they considered final? That is, were they founding law on justice or justification? political power on the power of Christ? Or were they not secretly building on another foundation, and, in so doing, in spite of all their apparent fidelity to the Bible, were they not actually either ignoring or misconstruing the fundamental truth of the Bible?

Let us consider what would happen if that were so: if the thought of human justice were merely clamped on to the truth of divine justification, instead of being vitally connected with it. On the one hand, to a certain extent it would be possible to purify the truth of divine justification from

[5] *Schlussreden*, Art. 35.

[6] Matthew 17, dealing as it does with a Temple tax, does not really belong here.

this foreign addition and to build upon it a highly spiritual message and a very spiritual Church, which would claim to expect "everything from God," in a most devout spirit, and yet, in actual fact, would dispute this "everything" because, by their exclusive emphasis upon the Kingdom of God, forgiveness of sins and sanctification, they had ceased to seek or find any entrance into the sphere of these problems of human justice. On the other hand, it would be possible to consider the question of human law very seriously (still, perhaps, in relation to the general divine providence, but freed from the Reformers' juxtaposition of human justice and divine justification) and to construct a secular gospel of human law and a secular church, in which, in spite of emphatic references to "God," it would inevitably become clear that this Deity is not the Father of our Lord Jesus Christ, and that the human justice which is proclaimed is in no sense the Justice of God. Since the Reformation it is evident that these two possibilities—and with them Pietistic sterility on one hand, and the sterility of the Enlightenment on the other—have been realized in many spheres. But it cannot be denied that there is a connection between this fact and that gap in the Reformers' teaching.

And now we live to-day at a time when, in the realm of the Church, the question of divine justification and, in the realm of the State, the question of human law are being raised with new emphasis, and we seem, now as then, to be pressing onward towards developments that cannot yet be foreseen. It is obvious to recall that both justification and justice, or the Kingdom of Christ and the kingdoms of this world, or the Church and the State, formerly stood side by side in the Reformation confession, and that by "worship in spirit and in truth" the Reformers understood a life in both these realms. But if we are not once more to drift into sterile and dangerous separations, it will not be enough to recollect the Reformation, to repeat the formulae in which it placed the two realms side by side, to recite over and again (with more or less historical accuracy and sympathetic feeling) "the Reformed conception of the State" and the like, as though that gap were not evident, as though the Reformation teaching did not, with that gap, bear within itself the temptation to those separations. If the intensity of our present situation is to be our salvation and not our ruin, then the question which we asked at the outset must be put: is there an actual, and therefore inward and vital, connection between the two realms?

What is offered here is a study—a biblical, or more exactly, a New Testament study—for the answer to this question. For the dubious character of the Reformation solution is decidedly due to the questionable character of the authoritative scriptural arguments on this subject presented at that time. If we are to progress further to-day, we must at all costs go back to the Scriptures. This pamphlet represents a partial attempt in this direction.[7]

I shall begin by reproducing in a few sentences what is, as far as I can see, the latest important statement of theological thought upon this subject: the work presented on our theme by K. L. Schmidt in his Basle inaugural lecture of December 2, 1936, under the title, "The Conflict of Church and State in the New Testament Community."[8]

[7] The reader will do well to note that in this book one thing only is attempted: to move along the road of exegesis towards a better view of the problem "Church and State." It would in my opinion be a great advantage if some were to admit that such an attempt is necessary.

[8] *Theologische Blätter*, 1937, No. 1. Since the completion of this work I have encountered Gerhard Rittel, *Das Urteil des neuen Testaments über den Staat* (*Zeitschr. f. Syst. Theol.*, 14 Jahrg. 1937, pp. 651–80, published in June 1938). It throws no new light on the subject with which I am concerned. On p. 665 of the essay we are asked to consider carefully "whether our exegesis is *true* exegesis, that is, whether its only goal is to discover what is given in the text or whether the writer's own wishes have—perhaps unconsciously—been introduced." Now this is a warning that can always be heard to advantage. Only we are also entitled to ask for some restraint in their apostrophizing of others from those who cannot themselves be certain as to what

The fundamental teaching of the Church on her relation to the State is "the harsh picture of the execution of Jesus Christ by the officials of the State." What is this State? It is one of those angelic powers (ἐξουσίαι) of this age, which is always threatened by "demonization," that is, by the temptation of making itself an absolute. And, over against this State, what is the Church? It is the actual community (πολίτευμα) of the new Heaven and the new Earth, as such here and now certainly still hidden, and therefore in the realm of the State a foreign community (παροικία). But the solidarity of distress and death unites Christians with all men, and so also with those who wield political power. Even though the Church prefers to suffer persecution at the hands of the State, which has become a "beast out of the pit of the abyss," rather than take part in the deification of Caesar, yet it still knows that it is responsible for the State and for Caesar, and it finally manifests this responsibility, "the prophetic service of the Church as Watchman," in its highest form by praying for the State and for its officials in all circumstances.

Schmidt's presentation is explicitly confined to one section only of the problem of the "Church and State in the New Testament," namely, with the question that appears to be directly opposed to ours: the question of the *conflict* between the two realms. But it seems to me important to determine that even in this other aspect of the problem, investigation of the New Testament inevitably reveals a whole series of view-points which are of the highest importance for the answer to our question about the *positive* connection between the two realms. This is so clear that in what follows I shall confine myself simply to the order traced by Schmidt.

---

they *must*, and what they *may not*, say on this subject. On p. 652, for example, the statements and the omissions on the subject of the "Fremdstaat" and the "Volksstaat" may well be as closely related to the "wishes" of the author as to those of certain "principalities and powers."

I. THE CHURCH AND THE STATE AS THEY
CONFRONT ONE ANOTHER

I, too, consider it right and important to point first of all to the situation in which *Jesus* and *Pilate* confront one another. So far as I can see, the Reformation writers in their teaching about Church and State, among all the somewhat significant Gospel texts that are concerned with this encounter, were interested only in the words of John 18:36: "My Kingdom is not of this world." Their thoughts about the Electoral Prince of Saxony or the Council of Zürich or Geneva would clearly have been disturbed, had they concentrated intensively upon the person of Pilate. But did the Reformers see clearly at this point? Is a "disturbance" all that can be expected? Might they not perhaps have found here a better foundation for what they wished to say on this matter? Here, at any rate, we must try to fill up the gap which they have left.[9]

[9] In the following passage I have found Calvin's views on the *sub Pontio Pilato* of the creed most illuminating. The passage is actually set in a quite different context.

Pourquoy n'est il dict simplement en un mot qu'il est mort, mais est parté de Ponce Pilate, soutsz lequel il a souffert?

Cela n'est pas seulement pour nous asseurer de la certitude de l'histoire: mais aussi pour signifier, que sa mort emporte condemnation.

Comment cela?

Il est mort, pour souffrir la peiene qui nous estoit deue, et par ce moyen nous en delivrer. Or pource que nous estions coulpables devant le jugement de Dieu comme mal-faicteurs: pour representer nostre personne, il a voulu comparoistre devant le siege d'un iuge terrien, et estre condamné par la bouche d'iceluy: pour nous absoudre au throne du Juge celeste.

Neantmoins Pilate le prononce innocent et ainsi il ne le condamné pas, comme s'il en estoit digne (Matth. xxvii. 24; Luc. xxiii. 14).

Il y a l'un et l'autre. C'est qu'il est justife par le temoignage du iuge, pour monstrer, qu'il ne souffre point pour ses demerites, mais pour les nostres: et cependant est condamné solennellement

In point of fact, in this encounter two points stand out with an almost blinding clarity: the State, in its "demonic" form, and thus its authority as the "power of the present age," on the one hand; the homelessness of the Church in this age, on the other hand. If the "rulers[10] of this world" had recognized the wisdom of God, which "we," the apostles, speak to the perfect, then "they would not have crucified the Lord of Glory" (I Corinthians 2:6 f.). There they showed that they did not recognize the wisdom of God. But the teaching on the separation between Church and State was not, and is not, the only teaching which the Church may glean from the passages concerned with the encounter between Jesus and Pilate.

I turn next to John 19:11; here Jesus expressly confirms Pilate's claim to have "power" over Him, and not, indeed, an accidental or presumptuous power, but one given to him "from above."[11] And this power is in no sense in itself, and as such, a power of the Evil One, of enmity to Jesus and His claims. Pilate himself formulated the matter thus in the

---

par la sentence d'iceluy mesme, pour denoter, qu'il est vrayment nostre pleige, recevant la condamnation pour nous afin de nous en acquiter.

C'est bien dit. Car s'il estoit pecheur il ne seroit pas capable de souffrir la mort pour les autres: et neantmoins, afin que sa condamnation nous soit delivrance, il faut qu'il soit repute entre les iniques (Jes. liii. 12).

Je l'entens ainsi.

(Catéchisme de l'Eglise de Genève, 1542. *Bekenntnisschriften der nach Gottes Wort reformierter Kirchen*, Munich, 1937 f. Vol. I., p. 9.)

[10] "Archontes" is the title given in Romans 13:3 to the officials of the State!

[11] In view of this passage, it seems to me impossible to say, as does Schlier (*Die Beurteilung des Staates im neuen Testament*, 1932, p. 312): "The earthly State cannot possibly pronounce judgment on this Kingdom and its representatives." It was clearly called to do so through the synagogue of the old Covenant (and, in the sense in which the Gospels use the words, it was certainly called to do so "non sine deo").

previous verse 10: "I have power to release thee and power to crucify thee." As power given by God, it could be used either way towards Jesus without losing its divine character. Certainly, had Jesus been released by Pilate, that would not have meant that the claim of Jesus to be King would have been recognized. Who for this end was born, and for this end came into the world, that He should bear witness to the truth (John 18:37). Such "recognition" cannot be and is not Pilate's business. To the question of truth, the State is neutral. "What is truth?" But the release of Jesus, and with it the recognition by the "rulers of this world" of the wisdom of God, might have meant the possibility of proclaiming openly the claim of Jesus to be such a king; or, in other words, it would have meant the legal granting of the right to preach justification! Now Pilate did *not* release Jesus. He used his power to crucify Jesus. Yet Jesus expressly acknowledged that even so his power was given him by God. Did He thereby, in the mind of the evangelist, subject Himself to the will and the verdict of a general divine providence? Or does the evangelist mean that in the use Pilate made of his power, instead of giving a just judgment, actually, under the cloak of legality, he allowed injustice to run its course? Was the one thing, or at least the chief thing, he wanted to emphasize here: that the State, by this decision, turned against the Church?

No; what he means is that what actually took place in this use of the statesman's power was the only possible thing that could take place in the fulfilment of the gracious will of the Father of Jesus Christ! Even at the moment when Pilate (still in the garb of justice! and in the exercise of the power given him by God) allowed injustice to run its course, he was the human created instrument of that justification of sinful man that was completed once for all time through that very crucifixion.

Consider the obvious significance of the whole process in the light of the Pauline message: when Pilate takes Jesus from the hands of the Jews in order to have Him scourged and crucified, he is, so to say, the middleman who takes Him over in the name of paganism, who in so doing declares the solidarity of paganism with the sin of Israel, but in so doing also enters into the inheritance of the promise made to Israel. What would be the worth of all the legal protection which the State could and should have granted the Church at that moment, compared with this act in which, humanly speaking, the Roman governor became the virtual founder of the Church? Was not this claim confirmed, for example, in the testimony of the centurion at the Cross (Mark 15:39) which anticipates all the creeds of Christendom? Then there is another truth which the Church might *also* gather from the meeting of Jesus and Pilate; namely, the very State which is "demonic" may will evil, and yet, in an outstanding way, may be constrained to do good. The State, even in this "demonic" form, cannot help rendering the service it is meant to render. It can no more evade it in the incident recorded by Luke 13:1–5, where the same Pilate, the murderer of young Galileans, becomes at the same time the instrument of the call to repentance, in the same way as the—equally murderous—Tower of Siloam. This is why the State cannot lose the honour that is its due. For that very reason the New Testament ordains that in all circumstances honour must be shown to its representatives (Romans 13:1–8; I Peter 2:17).

The synoptic accounts of the Barabbas episode point in the same direction. What is Pilate doing when he releases the "notable" Barabbas, cast into "prison for insurrection and murder," but delivers "to scourging and crucifixion" the Jesus whom he has himself declared to be guiltless? For all our amazement at such justice, we may not overlook the fact that in that very act of the political authority, not one of the earliest readers of the Gospels could think of anything other than that act of God, in which He "made Him to be sin for us, who knew no sin, that we might be made the righteousness of God in Him" (II Corinthians 5:21). What is this extremely unjust human judge doing at this point? In an eminent and direct way he is fulfilling the word of the supremely just Divine Judge. Where would the Church be if this released Barabbas were in the place of the guiltless Jesus? if, that is, there had been no "demonic" State?

Finally, there is one other point in the passages referring to Pilate which must not be overlooked: Jesus was *not* condemned as an enemy of the State, as the "King of the Jews" —although, according to Matthew 27:11; Mark 15:2, He acknowledged Himself to be a king.[12] Strictly speaking, Jesus was never condemned at all. All four evangelists vie with one another in contending that Pilate declared Him innocent, that he regarded Him as "a just man" (Matthew 27:19–24; Mark 15:14; Luke 23:14, 15, 22; John 18:38; 19:4, 6).[13] Here, too, the connection with justification now becomes clear: this same Pilate, constrained to become the instrument of the death of Jesus, ordained by God for the justification of sinful man—this same Pilate is also forced to confirm the presupposition of this event: to affirm expressly and openly the innocence of Christ, and—of course —it is in this very fact that he is fulfilling his specific function. "Pilate sought to release Him" (John 19:12). For it is in this sentence of acquittal (which he did *not* pro-

---

[12] It is not correct to say that Jesus "fell a victim to a political charge." (G. Dehn, "Engel und Obrigkeit," *Theologische Aufsätze*, 1936, p. 91.)

[13] I am indebted to Professor Ernst Wolf of Halle for the following: "On Ash Wednesday the Emperor kisses and gives gifts to the children of his orphanages; later in the procession, in the presence of the whole people, he enfeoffs or rather burdens the Minister of Justice with the 'Inkwell of Pilate,' and as he lays it on the neck of the bowing man he says 'Judge with justice like him.'" A direct reminder of the scrupulously correct behaviour of Roman justice in matters pertaining to this mystery did not seem to the successors in the Imperium Romanum out of place in Holy Week; to Syrians and Abyssinians the "Landpfleger" and his spouse Procla were almost holy beings. ("Sir Galahad," Byzanz. *Von Kaisern, Engeln und Eunuchen*, 1937, E. P. Tal and Co., Vienna, pp. 87–88.)

nounce) that his duty lies. If he had done so, the State would have shown its *true* face. Had it really done so, then acquittal would have had to follow, and the State would have had to grant legal protection to the Church! The fact that this did not actually happen is clearly regarded by the Evangelists as a deviation from the line of duty on the part of Pilate, as a failure on the part of the State. Pilate "delivered" Jesus to crucifixion, because he wished to satisfy the people (Mark 15:15). The political charge against Jesus was for Pilate clearly groundless, but he "gave sentence that it should be as they required" (Luke 23:24). "Take *ye* him and crucify him!" (John 19:6). This decision has nothing to do with the law of the State nor with the administration of justice. The Jews themselves confirmed this: "*We* have a law and by *our* law he ought to die" (John 19:7). It was not in accordance with the law of the State, but *in spite* of this law, and in accordance with a totally *different* law, and in flagrant defiance of justice, that Jesus had to die. "Ye, the Jews, have killed Jesus!" is the cry throughout the New Testament, with the exception of I Corinthians 2:8 (Acts 2:23; 3:15; 7:52; I Thessalonians 2:15). In this encounter of Pilate and Jesus the "demonic" State does not assert itself too much but too little; it is a State which at the decisive moment fails to be true to itself. Is the State here an absolute? If only Pilate had taken himself absolutely seriously as a representative of the State he would have made a different use of his power. Yet the fact that he used it as he did could not alter the fact that this power was really given him "from above." But he could not use it as he did without contradicting his true function; under the cloak of legality he trampled on the law which he should have upheld; in so doing, however, it became evident that if he had been true to his commission he would have had to decide otherwise. Certainly, in deflecting the course of justice he became the involuntary agent and herald of divine justification; yet at the same time he makes it clear that real human justice, a real exposure of the true face of the State, would inevitably have meant the recognition of the right to proclaim divine justification, the Kingdom of Christ which is not of this world, freely and deliberately.

We must not again lose sight of this doubly positive determination of the encounter between these two realms, as it has emerged in this critical instance. Particularly in considering this most critical instance we cannot say that the legal administration of the State "has nothing to do with the order of Redemption"; that here we have been moving in the realm of the first and not of the second article of the Creed.[14] No, Pontius Pilate now belongs not only to the Creed but to its second article in particular!

II. THE ESSENCE OF THE STATE

Turning to the exegesis of the passage Romans 13:1-7, which has been so much studied in every age, it may be thought peculiar that although an ancient explanation mentioned by Irenaeus[15] was clearly not generally accepted, yet in recent years fresh emphasis has been laid[16] on the fact that the word ἐξουσίαι, which is used by Paul in verse 1, and in Titus 3:1 and also by Luke, to indicate political authority is used throughout the rest of the New Testament, wherever it appears, in the plural (or in the singular with πᾶσα) (I Corinthians 15:24; Colossians 1:16; 2:10, 15; Ephesians 1:21; 3:10; 6:12; I Peter 3:22) to indicate a group of those angelic powers which are so characteristic of the biblical conception of the world and of man. ἐξουσίαι, like ἀρχαί or ἄρχοντες, δυνάμεις, θρόνοι, κυριότητες, ἄγγελοι, etc., and all these entities

[14] G. Dehn, op. cit., pp. 97 and 106.
[15] Adv. o.h. V. 24, I.
[16] Was H. Schlier ("Machte und Gewalten im neuen Testament," Theologische Blätter, 292) the first to express this? G. Dehn was in any case the first to develop the argument to any great extent.

which are so difficult to distinguish (probably they should all be included under the comprehensive heading ἄγγελοι) constitute created, but invisible, spiritual and heavenly powers, which exercise, in and above the rest of creation, a certain independence, and in this independence have a certain superior dignity, task, and function, and exert a certain real influence.

The researches of G. Dehn strengthen the already strong probability which arises from the language itself, that when the Church of the New Testament spoke of the State, the emperor or king, and of his representatives and their activities, it had in mind the picture of an "angelic power" of this kind, represented by this State and active within it. We have already met the concept ἐξουσία in the singular as indicating the power given to Pilate, to crucify Jesus or to release Him. Similarly, the concept ἄρχοντες (I Corinthians 2:8) is certainly intended to designate the State —and an angelic power.[17] What does this mean? It has been rightly maintained[18] that this explains how it came to pass that the State, from being the defender of the law, established by God's will and ordinance, could become "the beast out of the abyss" of Revelation 13,[19] dominated by the Dragon, demanding the worship of Caesar, making war on the Saints, blaspheming God, conquering the entire world. An angelic power may indeed become wild, degenerate, perverted, and so become a "demonic" power. That, clearly, had happened with the State as represented by Pilate which crucified Jesus. When Paul warns the Colossian Christians against the seductions of these angelic powers which have become "demonic," against a "worshipping of angels" (Colossians 2:18), when he exhorts them to

---

[17] And according to Rom. viii. 39 (οὔτε τις κτίσις ἑτέρα) we may not be far from the truth of the matter in describing the State as an ανθρωπίνη κτίσις (I Pet. ii. 13).

[18] Cf. G. Dehn, op. cit., p. 108.

[19] Cf. H. Schlier, "Vom Antichrist," *Theologische Aufsätze,* 1936, p. 110 f.

strive not with flesh and blood but with principalities and powers, with "rulers of the darkness of this world" (Ephesians 6:12), when he comforts them by the assurance that these "powers" cannot separate us from the love of Christ (Romans 8:38 f.),[20] and when he gives the vision of their ultimate "deliverance" through Christ in His parousia (I Corinthians 15:24)—all this may have a more or less direct bearing upon the "demons" and the "demonic" forces in the political sphere.

But the last passage which was quoted also contains a warning. When the separation between Christ and the State has been established, the last word on the vision of the "beast out of the abyss" has not been said. I think it is dangerous to translate the word καταργεῖν in I Corinthians 15:24 as "annihilate"—however clearly it bears that meaning in other passages. For immediately afterwards, in verse 25, the passage runs: "He must reign till He hath put all His enemies under His feet"—that is, till He has sovereign power over them. But that is also the image used in Philippians 2:9 f.—"Wherefore God also hath highly exalted Him, and given Him a name which is above every name; that at the name of Jesus every knee should bow, of things in Heaven and things in earth and things under the earth"; in Ephesians 1:20, 21—"He set Him at His own right hand in the heavenly places far above all principality and power and might. . . ."; in I Peter 3:22—"Who is gone into heaven and is on the right hand of God; angels and authorities and powers being made subject unto Him." The same image, too, is used in that particularly striking passage: Colossians 2:15: "Having spoiled principalities and powers, He made a show of them openly, triumphing over them in it." The destiny of the rebellious angelic powers which is made clear in Christ's resurrection and parousia is not that they will be annihilated, but that they will be forced into the service and the glorification of Christ, and,

[20] I am surprised that G. Dehn (op. cit., p. 101) maintains the opposite point of view.

through Him, of God. And both the beginning and the middle of their story also correspond to this ultimate destiny. I fail to see how one can say[21] without further ado that they simply represent "the world which lives on itself and by itself and as such is the antipodes and exact opposite of the creation": "In them the solitary world arises." According to Colossians 1:15 it is rather the case that they have been created in the Son of God as in the image of the invisible God, by Him and unto Him, and further, according to Colossians 2:10, that in Him they have their Head. From the first, then, they do not belong to themselves. From the first they stand at the disposal of Jesus Christ. To them, too, His work is relevant: "He was seen of angels" (I Timothy 3:16). The outcome of St. Paul's preaching to the heathen is that through the existence of the Church the "manifold wisdom of God"[22] might be made known unto them (Ephesians 3:10). With the Church they, too, desire to gaze into the mystery of the salvation which is to be revealed in the future (I Peter 1:12). And they are present not only as spectators; for them, too, the peace won by the crucifixion of Christ (Colossians 1:20) and the ἀνακεφαλαίωσις (Ephesians 1:10) are in both passages related both to earth and to heaven. We should note that here there is no question of any justification of the "demons" and the "demonic" forces; nor is the function of Christ concerning the angelic powers directly connected with divine justification. But it seems to have some connection with human justice. For what seems to be meant here is that in Christ the angelic powers are called to order and, so far as they need it, they are restored to their original order. Therefore any further rebellion in this realm can, in principle, only take place in accordance with their creation, and within Christ's order, in the form of unwilling service to the Kingdom of Christ, until even that rebellion, within the boundaries of the King-

---

[21] With H. Schlier, *Machte und Gewalten*, op. cit., p. 291.
[22] Probably Colossians 1:26 may also belong here.

dom of Christ, is broken down in His resurrection and
parousia. At the present time, in the period bounded by
the resurrection and the parousia, there is no further rebellion of the heavenly powers; no longer can they escape
from their original order.

What follows when all this is applied to the political
angelic power? Clearly this: that that power, the State as
such, belongs originally and ultimately to Jesus Christ; that
in its comparatively independent substance, in its dignity,
its function, and its purpose, it should serve the Person and
the Work of Jesus Christ and therefore the justification of
the sinner. The State can of course become "demonic," and
the New Testament makes no attempt to conceal the fact
that at all times the Church may, and actually does, have
to deal with the "demonic" State. From this point of view
the State becomes "demonic" not so much by an unwar-
rantable assumption of autonomy—as is often assumed—as
by the *loss* of its legitimate, relative *independence,* as by
a renunciation of its true substance, dignity, function, and
purpose, a renunciation which works out in Caesar worship,
the myth of the State, and the like. We should add that,
in the view of the New Testament, in *no* circumstances can
this "demonic" State finally achieve what it desires; with
gnashing of teeth it will have to serve where it wants to
dominate; it will have to build where it wishes to destroy;
it will have to testify to God's justice where it wishes to
display the injustice of men.

On the other hand, it is not inevitable that the State
should become a "demonic" force.[23] In the New Testament
it is not suggested that by its very nature, as it were, the
State will be compelled, sooner or later, to play the part

[23] Political events of the last decades have introduced into
New Testament exegesis on this matter a certain pessimism
which seems to me not to be justified by the actual facts of the
case. The State of Revelation 13 is, as H. Schlier (*Die Beurteilung
des Staates,* op. cit., p. 329) rightly maintains, "the borderline of
the possible State."

of "the Beast out of the abyss." Why should this be inevitable, since it, too, has been created in Christ, through Him and for Him, and since even to it the manifold wisdom of God is proclaimed by the Church? It could not itself become a Church, but from its very origin, in its concrete encounter with Christ and His Church, it could administer justice and protect the law (in accordance with its substance, dignity, function, and purpose, and in so doing remaining true to itself instead of losing itself!). In so doing, voluntarily or involuntarily, very indirectly yet none the less certainly, it would be granting the gospel of justification a free and assured course. In the light of the New Testament doctrine of angels, it is impossible to ignore the fact that the State may also manifest its neutral attitude towards Truth, by rendering to the Church, as a true and just State, that service which lies in its power to render; by granting it its true and lawful freedom, "that we may lead a quiet and peaceable life in all godliness and honesty" (I Timothy 2:2). If, even when it has become an unjust State and a persecutor of the Church, it cannot escape the real subordination in which it exists, yet in the same real subordination it may also show its true face as a just State (in practice, that may well mean at least a part of its true face) as, indeed, it appears to have manifested it to a great extent in all that concerns Paul, according to the Acts of the Apostles.[24]

Thus there is clearly no cause for the Church to act as though it lived, in relation to the State, in a night in which all cats are grey. It is much more a question of continual decisions, and therefore of distinctions between one State

[24] Up to the present, the κατέχον and κατέχων of II Thessalonians 2:6 ff. have been taken to indicate that function of the Roman State which works against the Antichrist. Had this interpretation not been "unfortunately" shattered by O. Cullmann, this passage would also have to be considered here. (*Le caractère eschatologique du devoir missionaire et de la conscience apostolique de St. Paul.* Recherches théologiques, Strasbourg, 1936, pp. 26–61.)

and another, between the State of yesterday and the State of to-day. According to I Corinthians 12:10 the Church receives, among other gifts, that of "discerning of spirits." If by these "spirits" we are to understand the angelic powers, then they have a most significant political relevance in preaching, in teaching, and in pastoral work.

One decisive result of this exegesis as a whole should be a clear understanding of the meaning of Romans 13. The God from Whom all this concrete authority comes, by Whom all powers that be are ordained (v. 1), Whose ordinance every man resists who resists that power (v. 2), Whose διάκονος it is (v. 4), and Whose λειτουργοί its representatives are (v. 6)—this God cannot be understood apart from the Person and the Work of Christ; He cannot be understood in a general way as Creator and Ruler, as was done in the expositions of the Reformers, and also by the more recent expositors up to and including Dehn and Schlier. When the New Testament speaks of the State, we are, fundamentally, in the *Christological* sphere; we are on a lower level than when it speaks of the Church, yet, in true accordance with its statements on the Church, we are in the same unique Christological sphere. It is not sufficient to state[25] that the ὑπὸ θεοῦ sweeps away all hypotheses which suggest that the origin of the State is in nature, in fate, in history, or in a social contract of some kind, or in the nature of society, and the like; this, too, is why it is not sufficient to state that the foundation of the State reminds it of its limits. The phrase ὑπὸ θεοῦ does mean this, it is true, but it must be added that in thus stating this foundation and limitation of the State, Paul is not thinking of some general conception of God, in the air, so to speak, but he is indicating Him in Whom all the angelic powers have their foundation and their limits, the "image of the invisible God" Who as such is also "the first-born of all creation" (Colossians 1:15). We need only see

25 With H. Schlier, *Die Beurteilung des Staates,* op. cit., p. 323.

that for Paul, within the compass of *this* centre and therefore *within* the Christological sphere (although outside the
sphere characterized by the word "justification"), there was
embodied in the angelic world another secondary Christological sphere—if I may put it so—uniting the Church with
the Cosmos, wherein the necessity and the reality of the
establishment and administration of human justice were
clearly important above all else—thus we need only see this
in order to note that in Romans 13 the Name of God is
used in a very clear way, and not in any vague manner.
The establishment and the function of the State, and, above
all, the Christian's attitude towards it, will then lose a certain accidental character which was peculiar to the older
form of exposition. We shall then not have to relate to God,
as distinct from Jesus Christ, the grounds for the attitude
required by I Peter 2:13, "for the Lord's sake"[26]; just as in
the use of similar formulae in the epistles to the Colossians
and the Ephesians, according to the specific witness of Colossians 3:24 and Ephesians 5:20; 6:6, no other "Lord" is
meant than Jesus Christ. "Submitting yourselves one to another in the fear of *Christ*" (Ephesians 5:21, R. V.). It is
the fear of Christ—that is, the sense of indebtedness to Him
as the Lord of all created lords (Colossians 4:1; Ephesians
6:9) which would be dishonoured by an attitude of hos-
tility, and it is the fear of Christ which clearly, according
to I Peter 2:13 f., forms the foundation for the imperative:
"Submit yourselves . . . to the King." And we shall have
to think in the same direction when in Romans 13:5 it is
claimed of the same submission that it should occur not
merely through anxiety before the wrath of authority but
for conscience' sake. Συνείδησις (conscience) means
"to know with." With *whom* can man *know something?*
The New Testament makes this quite clear. Schlatter has
translated the συνείδησις θεοῦ of I Peter 2:19 as "certainty
of God." It is clear that in I Corinthians 10:25–27, where the

[26] With G. Dehn, op. cit., p. 99.

formula used in Romans 13:5 also appears, it does not indicate a norm imposed upon mankind in general but one imposed on the Christian in particular—and that from the recognition of that norm implies that he must adopt a definite attitude. Christian knowledge, Christian certainty, and the Christian conscience do not demand that Christians should enquire in the shambles or at the feast about the origin of the meat that is set before them (I Corinthians 10). But the Christian conscience does demand that they should submit to authority (Romans 13). Clearly this is because in this authority we are dealing indirectly, but in reality, with the authority of Jesus Christ.

III. THE SIGNIFICANCE OF THE STATE
FOR THE CHURCH

In order to throw light upon the contrast between Church and State emphasis has always, rightly, been laid on the fact that the State (πολίτευμα) or the city (πόλις) of Christians should not be sought in the "present age" but in that "which is to come"; not on earth but in heaven. That is, in an impressive way, the theme of Philippians 3:20; Hebrews 11:10, 13–16; 12:22; 13:14. And in Revelation 21 this city of the Christians is surveyed and presented, with its walls, gates, streets, and foundations: "The holy city, new Jerusalem, coming down from God out of heaven, prepared as a bride adorned for her husband" (v. 2). In this city there is, strikingly, no temple: "For the Lord God the Almighty, and the Lamb, are the temple thereof" (v. 22). That is why it is said: "The nations shall walk in the light of it: and the kings of the earth do bring their glory and honour into it. And the gates of it shall not be shut at all by day: (for there shall be no night there). And they shall bring the glory and honour of the nations into it. And there shall in no wise enter into it anything that defileth, neither whatsoever worketh abomination or maketh a lie; but they which are written in the Lamb's book of life" (v. 24-27). It must here be emphasized, above all else, that in this future city in which Christians have their citizenship here and now (without yet being able to inhabit it), we are concerned not with an ideal but with a real State—yes, with the only real State; not with an imaginary one but with the only one that truly exists. And it is the fact that Christians have their citizenship in this, the real State, that makes them strangers and sojourners within the State, or within the States of this age and this world. Yes, if they are "strangers and pilgrims" here it is because this city constitutes below their faith and their hope—and not because they see the imperfections or even the perversions of the states of this age and this world! It is not resentment, but a positive sentiment, through which, in contradistinction to non-Christians, it comes about, that they have "no continuing city" here (Hebrews 13:14). It is because Paul knows that he is "garrisoned" by the Peace of God which passes all understanding, that the *Pax Romana* cannot impress Paul as an "ultimate."[27] It is because "the saints shall judge the world"—and not because the Corinthian law-courts were particularly bad—that, according to I Corinthians 6:1-6, Christians must be able, within certain limits, to renounce their right to appeal to the law of the State and its courts of justice.

It is the hope of the new age, which is dawning in power, that separates the Church from the State, that is, from the States of this age and this world. The only question is whether this same hope does not also in a peculiar way unite the two. H. Schlier,[28] who rightly answers the question in the affirmative, describes this bond as follows: "Whoever considers human life as ordered and established in faith, for this world which God is preparing . . . in face of the claims of the actual earthly bonds, and in the claims of the most exacting of all bonds—that of the State—will discern in them the will of God, and will see bonds estab-

[27] Cf. K. L. Schmidt, *Theologische Blätter*, 1937, No. 1, p. 8.
[28] *Die Beurteilung des Staates*, op. cit., p. 320.

lished by God. In the eschatological knowledge about the actual end of the world, the present world is proclaimed in its real and true character as the creation of God's word." To that I would like to ask whether the New Testament anywhere shows any interest in the "present world in its real and true character as the creation of God" save in so far as it finds it to be grounded, constituted, and restored in Christ? In this case, when we think of this bond, should we not do better to look forward, to the coming age, to Christ? rather than backward—that is, rather than think in the abstract about creation and the hypothetic divine bonds established by this creation.

Of one thing in the New Testament there can be no doubt: namely, that the description of the order of the new age is that of a *political* order. Think of the significant phrase: the Kingdom of God, or of Heaven, that it is called *Kingdom* of God or Heaven, and remember, too, the equally "political" title of the King of this realm: *Messias* and *Kyrios*. And from Revelation 21 we learn that it is not the real church (ἐκκλησία) but the real city (πόλις) that truly constitutes the new age. Or, to put it otherwise, the Church sees its future and its hope, not in any heavenly image of its own existence but in the real heavenly *State*. Wherever it believes in, and proclaims here and now, the justification of the sinner through the blood of the Lamb, it will see before it, "coming down out of Heaven from God," the city of eternal *law* in which there is no offender and whose doors need never be closed, but which also needs no temple, for the same Lamb will be its temple. And this city will not endure merely on the ruins of the annihilated glory of the peoples and the kings of this earth, but the whole of this earthly glory will be brought into it, as supplementary tribute. Could the Church of divine justification hold the human law-State in higher esteem than when it sees in that very State, in its heavenly reality, into which its terrestrial existence will finally be absorbed, the final predicate of its own grounds for hope? Deification of the

State then becomes impossible, not because there is no divinity of the State, but because it is the divinity of the *heavenly* Jerusalem, and as such cannot belong to the *earthly* State. But the opposite of such deification, which would consist of making the State a devil, is also impossible. We have no right to do as Augustine liked to do, and straightway identify the *civitas terrena* with the *civitas Cain.* Not because its representatives, office-bearers, and citizens can protect it from becoming the State of Cain, or even of the devil, but because the heavenly Jerusalem is also a State, and every State, even the worst and most perverse, possesses its imperishable destiny in the fact that it will one day contribute to the glory of the heavenly Jerusalem, and will inevitably bring its tribute thither.

From this point of view we can understand two passages from the Epistle to the Ephesians, in which the writer—although the word of the Kingdom of God which is not of this world was known to him, if not in those actual words, at least in reality—has no hesitation in describing the Church itself (in a connection in which he is considering its earthly and temporal reality) as the commonwealth of Israel (Ephesians 2:12) and later describes its members (in contradistinction to their past nature as strangers and foreigners) as fellow-citizens with the saints (Ephesians 2:19). There is no need to labour the point that this "politicizing" of the earthly Church is "from above," affirmed from the point of view of the ultimate reality, of the "last things," which, however, neither removes nor alters the fact that in this age, and in relation to the State, the Church is a "stranger." But, for that very reason, it is remarkable that the concepts, so important for the Christians, of "strangers and foreigners" are used to describe those who do not belong to the Church, and that the concept of the "rights of citizenship," so important for the ancient State, can become the predicate of the Church on earth. Here, too, we must ask whether the objection of the early Christians to the earthly State, and the consciousness of being "strangers" within this

State, does not mean essentially that this State has been too little (and not too much!) of a State for those who know of the true State in heaven; or, again, we might put the question positively, and ask whether, in view of the basis and origin of the earthly State, these Christians have not seen, in the Gospel of divine justification, the infinitely better, the true and only real source and norm of all human law, even in this "present age." The desire or the counsel of Paul, in I Corinthians 6:1–6, which so clearly points to something like legislation within the Church itself would otherwise be incomprehensible.

It is essential that we should arrive at this point—one might almost say at this prophecy: that it is the preaching of justification of the Kingdom of God, which founds, here and now, the true system of law, the true State. But it is equally essential that when this prophecy has been made, the Church on earth should not go beyond its own bounds and endow itself with the predicates of the heavenly State, setting itself up in concrete fashion against the earthly State as the true State. That it could and should do so cannot possibly be the meaning of Ephesians 2 and I Corinthians 6, because for the New Testament the *heavenly* State is and remains exclusively the *heavenly* State, established not by man but by God, which, as such, is not capable of realization in this age, not even in the Church. It was from the point of view of a later age that Clement of Alexandria[29] extolled the Church guided by the Logos as unconquered, enslaved by no arbitrary power, and even identical with the will of God on earth as in heaven; and again, later still, Augustine[30] was able to make the proud statement: "True justice is not to be found except in that republic, whose founder and ruler is Christ." It could be no accident that the writers of the Epistle to the Hebrews and the First Epistle of Peter neglected to console the Christians who were so homeless in this age and in this world by assuring

29 *Strom.* IV., 171, 2.
30 *De civ. Dei* II., 21.

them that nevertheless they had a home, here and now, in the Church. It is far more true that they have here *no* abiding city, and that the earthly Church stands over against the earthly State as a sojourning (παροικία) and not as a State within the State, or even as a State above the State, as was later claimed by the papal Church of Rome, and widened also by many a fanatical sect.

There are other conclusions to be drawn from Ephesians 2 and I Corinthians 6. This παροικία, this "establishment among strangers," does not wait for the city which is to come without doing anything. What indeed does take place in this παροικία? We might reply, simplifying, but not giving a wrong turn to the phrase: the preaching of justification. It is in this preaching that this "foreign community" affirms its hope in the city which is to come: in this preaching, that is, in the message which proclaims that by grace, and once for all, God has gathered up sinful man in the Person of Jesus, that He has made sin and death His own, and thus that He has not merely acquitted man, but that for time and for eternity He has set him free for the enjoyment of the life which he had lost. What the παροικία believes is simply the reality of this message, and what it hopes for is simply the unveiling of this reality, which still remains, here and now, concealed. We must note that it is not man or humanity, but the Lamb, the Messiah, Jesus, who is the Spouse for whom the Bride, the heavenly city, is adorned. It is He, and His Presence, as "the Lamb that hath been slain," who makes this City what it is, the City of Eternal Law. It is *His* law, the rights won by Jesus Christ in His death and proclaimed in His Resurrection which constitute this Eternal law. (Here we are confronted by a quite different conception from the Stoic conception of the "City" to which Clement of Alexandria refers in the passage which we have mentioned.) Now this eternal law of Jesus Christ constitutes precisely the content of the message of justification, in which, here and now, the task of the Church consists. The Church cannot itself effect the disclosure of this eternal law, neither in its own members nor in the world. It cannot anticipate the "Marriage of the Lamb" (Revelation 19:7). It cannot will to celebrate it in this "present age" but it can and it should proclaim it.

But—here we go a step further—it can and should proclaim it to the world. It is worth noticing that in all those passages in the Epistles that are directly concerned with our problem a window is thrown open in this direction, which, at first sight, seems somewhat strange. The behaviour towards the State which they demand from all Christians is always connected with their behaviour towards *all* men. "Render therefore to all their dues. . . . Owe *no man* anything but (which you can only do within the Church) to love one another" (Romans 13:7, 8). In I Timothy 2:1 we read that they should make "supplications, prayers, intercessions and giving of thanks for *all* men," and in Titus 3:2, immediately after the words on those in authority, we read "be gentle, showing all meekness unto *all* men." Finally in I Peter 2:13 we are again dealing with the "*Every* ordinance of man," and later in verse 17, going a step further (and here too in clear distinction to the love of the brotherhood) "honour all men." What does this mean? It seems to me, when considered in connection with I Timothy 2:1–7, that it clearly means this: since it is our duty to pray for all men, so we should pray in particular for kings and for all in authority, because it is only on the condition that such men exist that we can "lead a quiet and peaceable life in all godliness and honesty." Why is it necessary that we should be able to lead such a life? Are we justified[31] in interpolating at this point the words "as citizens," and so causing Christians to pray for the preservation of a sort of bucolic existence? The passage quite clearly goes on to say: "For this (obviously the possibility of our quiet and peaceable life) is good and acceptable in the sight of God our Saviour, who will have all men to be saved, and to come

[31] With H. Schlier, *Die Beurteilung des Staates*, op. cit., p. 325.

unto the knowledge of the truth. For there is *one* God, and *one* mediator between God and men, the man Christ Jesus; who gave Himself a ransom for all, to be testified in due time. Whereunto I am ordained a preacher and an apostle." Thus the quiet and peaceable life under the rule of the State, for the sake of which this passage calls us to pray for statesmen, is no ideal in itself, just as the existence of the Church, in contradistinction to all other men, can be no ideal in itself. It is the preacher and apostle who stands in need of this quiet and peaceable life, and this apostle, and with him stand those with whom he here identifies himself, not in the service of a Universal Creator and Preserver, but in the service of the Saviour, God, who will "have all men to be saved and to come unto the knowledge of the truth," who is the one God in the one Mediator, who gave Himself a ransom for all. Why does the community need "a quiet and peaceable life"? It needs it because in its own way, and in its own place, it likewise needs the preacher and apostle for all, and because it needs freedom in the realm of all men in order to exercise its function towards all men. But this freedom can only be guaranteed to it through the existence of the earthly State which ordains that all men shall live together in concord. Is not the argument for submission to the civil administration of justice given in I Peter 2:15 f., by the statement that it is the will of God that the Christians, as those who are recognized by law as well-doers, "may put to silence the ignorance of foolish men—as free and not using their liberty" guaranteed by the State "for a cloak of maliciousness," but will act in this freedom as servants of God? Since this freedom of the Church can only be guaranteed through the existence of the State, therefore there is no alternative but that the Church should on its side guarantee the existence of the State through its prayers. That this mutual guarantee can and should fundamentally be only temporary—that is, that by its very nature it can and should be exercised only in this age and in this world, that the State can and should only partially grant or totally deny the guarantee that the Church demands of it, that, finally, the Church cannot and should not require of the State any guarantee as to the validity or the effectiveness of its gospel—all this is not the least altered by the fact that the Church in all earnestness expects this *limited* guarantee from the State, nor by the fact that this guarantee which the Church requires of the State is a serious one and, as such, cannot be too seriously laid upon the hearts of its members. Prayer for the bearers of State authority belongs to the very essence of its own existence. It would not be a Church if it were to ignore this apostolic exhortation. It would then have forgotten that it has to proclaim this promised justification to *all* men.

But we must also understand the demand for loyalty to the State in the other passages in the epistles which deal with this subject in the light of I Timothy 2, that is, in the light of this mutual guarantee. In Titus 3:1–8, astonishingly enough, it is connected with the rebirth through baptism and the Holy Spirit. But that is not astonishing if the future heirs of eternal life, justified, according to verse 7, by the grace of Jesus Christ, receive all that not for themselves, but in the Church and as members of the Church for *all* men, and thus stand in need of freedom not for themselves but for the word of the Church and therefore for human law, and so have to respect the bearers and representatives of that law. And when, in Romans 13:3–4 and I Peter 2:14, we read that obedience must be rendered to authority because it is the duty of authority to reward the good and to punish the evil, then in the context of both epistles it seems to me an impossible interpretation to say that the writers were speaking of "good" and "evil" in a quite general and neutral sense, and that the justice of the State is equally general and neutral. Why should not the writers have been making the same use of these concepts as they did elsewhere and been demanding that Christians should do the good work of their faith, in the performance of which they, in contradistinction to the evildoers, have in no sense to fear the power of the State, but rather to expect its praise? Why, thinking of the "power" that was so clearly granted to Pilate to crucify or release Jesus, should they not first of all have pointed Christians to the better— i.e., the only true—possibility of the State, the possibility granted to it by the "good," i.e., by the Church, to protect the law (or, in other words, the possibility of a "Concordat"!)? The fact that the State could actually make use of the other possibility, that it could actually honour the evil and punish the good, may be quite true, but it cannot alter its mission, hence it does not affect the Christian attitude towards the State. Should the State go so far as to honour evildoers and to punish the good, if it can be recalled at all to its mission, and thereby to its own true possibility, it will be due to the Christian attitude towards it. And even if the State betrays its divine calling, it will nevertheless be constrained to fulfil its function, to guarantee the freedom of the Church, even if in a quite different way! The "honour" that the State owes to the Church will then consist in the suffering of the followers of Christ, described in the First Epistle of Peter:—and the punishment of the evildoers will then consist in the fact that the glory of this suffering will be withheld from them. Thus in one way or another the State will have to be the servant of divine justification.

Thus it is clear that in this very close relation between the existence of the Church and that of the State, the Church cannot itself become a State, and the State, on the other hand, cannot become a Church. It is true, of course, that in principle the Church, too, turns to all men; but it does so with its message of justification and its summons to faith. The Church gathers its members through free individual decisions, behind which stands the quite different free choice of God, and in this age it will never have to reckon with gathering all men within itself. The Church must have complete confidence in God, who is the God of *all* men, and must leave all to Him. But the State has always assembled within itself all men living within its boundaries, and it holds them together, as such, through its order, which is established and maintained by force. The State as State knows nothing of the Spirit, nothing of love, nothing of forgiveness. The State bears the sword, and at the best, as seen in Romans 13, it does not wield it in vain. It, too, must leave to God the question of what must be done for man's welfare, in addition to the administration of the law which is based on force. The State would be denying its own existence if it wished to become a Church. And the Church on its side, for its own sake, or rather, for the sake of its mission, can never wish that the State should cease to be the State. For it can never become a true Church. If it were insane enough to attempt this, it could only become an idolatrous Church. And, on the other hand, the Church would be denying its own existence if it wished to become a State and to establish law by force, when it should be preaching justification. It could not be a true State; it could only be a clerical State, with a bad conscience on account of its neglected duty, and incapable, on this foreign soil, of administering justice to all men, as is the duty of the State.

But this relation between the Church and the State does not exclude—but includes—the fact that the *problem* of the State, namely, the problem of law, is raised, and must be answered, within the sphere of the Church on Earth. Those phrases in Ephesians 2 are no mere rhetorical flourishes, but they are concretely related to the fact that there is and must be within the Church itself (and here its close relation to the State asserts itself) *something like* (I am here deliberately using an indefinite phrase) a commonwealth: with its offices and orders, divisions of labour and forms of community. This is known as *Ecclesiastical Law*. It is well known that Rudolf Sohm regarded the appearance of ecclesiastical law (which, according to him, took place only in the second century) as the great sin of the early Church. But the Christian Church of the first century, as pictured by Sohm, moved freely by the Spirit of God, hither and thither, never actually existed. Now there is *one* fundamental ecclesiastical principle which cannot be denied without at the same time denying the resurrection of Christ and, in so doing, the very heart of the entire New Testament: the authority of the apostolate. And from the start there arose from this one principle many others, in freedom indeed, but in the freedom of the Word of God, and in no other freedom. The words of Paul (I Corinthians 14:33) about the God who is the author not of confusion but of peace, and above all the whole argument of I Corinthians 12–14, are characteristic at this point. How could the Church expect law from the State and at the same time exclude law from its own life? How could it, and how can it, live out the teaching with which it has been entrusted and yet, in its own realm, dispense with law and order, with the order which serves to protect that teaching? Certainly, in the primitive Church there was not more than "something like a commonwealth"; it was certainly never a juridical community employing the methods of compulsion characteristic of the State; and when, later on, it became such a body it was to its own undoing. Ecclesiastical authority is spiritual authority—authority, that is, which implies the witness of the Holy Spirit. Does this make it less strict? Is it not for that very reason the strictest authority of all? Was there ever a more compelling legal order than that which we find presupposed in the letters of the Apostles?

But the other side of the question, in this connection, is still more remarkable: this antagonistic relation between Church and State does not exclude—on the contrary, it includes—the fact that the New Testament, if we examine it closely, in no sense deals with the order of the State, and the respect that is due to such an order, as something which affects the life of the Christian community only from without, but to *a certain extent* (and again I am deliberately using an indefinite phrase) the New Testament deals with it as the question of a kind of annexe and outpost of the

Christian community, erected in the world outside, which thus, in a certain sense, is included within the ecclesiastical order as such. The fact that the Church has had to assume a "certain" political character is balanced by the fact that the Church must recognize, and honour, a "certain" ecclesiastical character in the State. At all times, indeed, forms of "State Church" have always existed, which, in this respect at least, were not so far removed from the New Testament picture of things as might appear at first glance. It should be noted that the exhortation on the subject of the State in Romans 13 cannot possibly, if taken in its context, be regarded as an exceptional statement dealing with the Law of Nature, because it is firmly embedded in the midst of a series of instructions all of which have as their presupposition and their aim the Christian existence as such. In the First Epistle to Timothy it stands at the head of a series of exhortations dealing with the conduct of men and of women during worship, and with the office of the bishop and of the deacon. In the Epistle to Titus it stands at the end, and in the First Epistle of Peter at the beginning, of a similar series. The verb "be subject unto," so characteristic of the imperative of this exhortation (Romans 13:1; Titus 3:1; I Peter 2:13), is used not only in Titus 2:9 and I Peter 2:18 for the conduct of Christian slaves towards their masters but also in Colossians 3:18, Ephesians 5:22, Titus 2:5, and I Peter 3:1, 5 for the conduct of women towards men, in I Peter 5:5 for the conduct of the younger towards the older members of the community, and in Ephesians 5:21 and I Peter 5:5 for the conduct of Christians towards one another within the Church.

How do the "higher powers," the "rulers," the king and his governors come into this society? Does not the fact that they are within this society clearly show that this is a specifically *Christian* exhortation, that the secular authority and our attitude to it are to some extent included in those "orders" in which Christians have to prove their obedience to God? and indeed to the God who is revealed in Jesus

Christ? And what shall we say to the fact that the State
ruler in Romans 13:4 is characterized as the minister of
God, and the State officials in Romans 13:6, with their various demands on the public, as God's ministers?[32] How do
they come to receive this sacred name? It seems to me
clear that they do "to a certain extent" actually stand within
the sacred order, not—as was later said, with far too great
a servility—as *membra prœcipua*, but as *ministri extraor-
dinarii ecclesiœ*.

The light which falls from the heavenly polis upon the
earthly *ecclesia* is reflected in the light which illuminates
the earthly polis from the earthly *ecclesia*, through their
mutual relation. If the question of how this mutual relation
can be explained is not actually answered by I Timothy 2
coupled with Revelation 21, then a better explanation
would have to be found. But in any case, as such, the phe-
nomenon cannot well be denied.

IV. THE SERVICE WHICH THE CHURCH OWES
TO THE STATE

If we review the New Testament exhortations to Christians
on the subject of their relation to the State, we are certainly justified in placing intercession (I Timothy 2) in a
central position, as being the most intimate of all, and the
one which includes all others. But we must be careful to
see just how all-inclusive this particular exhortation is.
Christians are called to offer "supplications, prayers, intercessions and thanksgivings" for all men, and in particular
for kings and all who are in positions of authority. Does
the passage actually say less than this: that the Church
has (not as one incidental function among others, but in
the whole essence of its existence as a Church) to offer it-

[32] In Romans 15:16 and Philippians 2:25, Paul describes
himself and his fellow worker Epaphroditus as λειτουργὸν Ἰησοῦ
χριστοῦ εἰς τὰ ἔθνη; in Hebrews 1:2 the name is given to the
angels of God and in Hebrews 8:2 to Christ Himself!

self to God for all men, and in particular for the bearers of State power? But this "offering oneself for" all men means (for that is the significance of the ὑπέρ) that the Church is fulfilling, on its side, that worship of God which men cannot and will not accomplish, yet which must be accomplished. This intercession is necessary because from God alone can rulers receive and maintain that power which is so salutary for the Church and, for the sake of the preaching of justification, so indispensable to all men. Far from being the *object* of worship, the State and its representatives need prayer *on their behalf*. In principle, and speaking comprehensively, this is the essential service which the Church owes to the State. This service includes all others. In so doing, could the Church more clearly remind the State of its limits? or more clearly remind itself of its own freedom? than in thus offering itself on its behalf?

But this service must of course be rendered without asking whether the corresponding service owed by the State to the Church is also being given, and indeed without inquiring whether the individual bearers of State power are worthy of it. How could such inquiry be made before rendering a service of this kind? Clearly the service becomes all the more necessary the more negative the answer to the question; just as the nature of justification comes out still more clearly when we see that he who is "justified" is evidently a real and thorough sinner in the sight of God and man. Thus the more negative the answer to this question, the more urgently necessary is the priestly duty laid upon the Church; the most brutally unjust State cannot lessen the Church's responsibility for the State; indeed, it can only increase it.

Our understanding of "Be in subjection. . . ." in Romans 13:1 f. and the other passages would have been better served if we had not regarded this particular exhortation in the abstract, but had considered it in its relationship to this first, primary exhortation. Can this "subjection," fundamentally, mean anything other than the practical behaviour on the part of the members of the Church which corresponds to the priestly attitude of the Church as such? "Be subject unto" (ὑποτασσεδθαί) does not mean directly and absolutely "to be subject to someone," but to respect him as his office demands. We are here dealing with a subjection that is determined and conditioned by the framework within which it takes place, namely, by a definite τάξις (order). But the τάξις (as in other passages in which the word occurs) is not set up by the persons concerned who are to be the objects of respect, but, according to verse 2, it is based on the ordinance of God. It is on the basis, then, of this divine ordinance that such respect must be shown. But in what way can this due respect be shown to the leaders of the State, unless Christians behave towards it in the attitude of mind which always expects the best from it—expects, that is, that it will grant legal protection to the free preaching of justification—but which is also prepared—under certain circumstances—to carry this preaching into practice by suffering injustice instead of receiving justice, and thereby acknowledging the State's power to be, in one way or another, God-given? If Christians were not to do this, if they were to oppose this ordinance and thus to refuse the State authority the respect which is determined and limited by divine decree, then, according to verse 2, they would be opposing the will of God, and their existence within the sphere of the State would become their condemnation. If they neither reckoned with this positive divine claim of the State nor were prepared, if need be, to suffer injustice at its hands, then by that very fact they would belong to those evil ones who must fear its power, and towards whom, by the use of its sword and the power of compulsion that is granted to it, it could only, openly or secretly ("power as such is evil"), be the force which executes the divine wrath, the dread manifestation of the perdition of this age (verses 4–5).

But this respect for the authority of the State which is demanded in Romans 13 must not be separated—in theory or in practice—from the priestly function of the Church. It cannot possibly consist of an attitude of abstract and absolute elasticity towards the intentions and undertakings of the State, simply because, according not only to the Apocalypse but also to Paul, the possibility may arise that the power of the State, on its side, may become guilty of opposition to the Lord of lords, to that divine ordinance to which it owes its power. If Christians are still to respect the State, even then, their docility in this instance can only be passive and, as such, limited. The "subjection" can in no case mean that the Church and its members will approve, and wish of their own free will to further, the claims and undertakings of the State, if once the State power is turned not to the protection but to the suppression of the preaching of justification. Even then, Christians will never fail to grant that which is indispensable to the State power as guardian of the public law, as an ordained power—"tribute to whom tribute is due, custom to whom custom, fear to whom fear, honour to whom (as representative and bearer of ἐξουσία) honour—even if the State abuses this ἐξουσία and demonstrates its opposition, as a demonic power, to the Lord of lords. Even then, according to Matthew 22:21, Christians will render unto Caesar the things which are Caesar's, i.e., whatever is his due, not as a good or a bad Caesar, but simply as Caesar; the right which is his, even if he turns that right to wrong. As has been shown, it is and remains a God-established ἐξουσία, and that which we owe it, even then, must not be withheld. But the fact also remains, unalterably, that Christians are to render unto God the things which are God's; and likewise, that the Church must be and must remain the Church. Thus the "subjection" required of Christians can *not* mean that they accept and take upon themselves responsibility for those intentions and undertakings of the State which directly or indirectly are aimed against the freedom of preaching. Of course it must be understood that even then the "subjection" will not cease. But their submission, their *respect* for the power of the State to which they continue to give what they owe, will consist in becoming its victims, who, in their concrete action will not accept any responsibility, who cannot inwardly co-operate, and who as "subjects" will be unable to conceal the fact, and indeed ought to express it publicly, in order that the preaching of justification may be continued under all circumstances. All this will be done, not *against* the State, but as the Church's service *for* the State! Respect for the authority of the State is indeed an annexe to the priestly function of the Church towards the State. Christians would be neglecting the distinctive service which they can and must render to the State, were they to adopt an attitude of unquestioning assent to the will and action of the State which is directly or indirectly aimed at the suppression of the freedom of the Word of God. For the possibility of intercession for the State stands or falls within the freedom of God's Word. Christians would, in point of fact, become enemies of any State if, when the state threatens their freedom, they did *not* resist, or if they concealed their resistance—although this resistance would be very calm and dignified. Jesus would, in actual fact, have been an enemy of the State if He had *not* dared, quite calmly, to call King Herod a "fox" (Luke 13:32). If the State has perverted its God-given authority, it cannot be honoured better than by this *criticism* which is due to it in all circumstances. For this power that has been perverted, what greater service can we render than that of intercession? Who can render this service better than the Christian? And how could Christians intercede, if, by themselves acquiescing in the perversion of the power of the State, they had become traitors to their own cause? And where would be their respect for the State if it involved such betrayal?

Through this discussion of the "subjection" of Romans 13:1 (in its connection with I Timothy 2:1), we have gained a fundamental insight into the nature of the service which the Church, as the organ of divine justification, owes to the State, as the organ of human law, which the State has a right to expect from it, and by which, if it remains obedient, it can actually assist the State. We have affirmed that there is a mutual guarantee between the two realms. We now ask: what is the guarantee which the Church has to offer to the State?

After all that we have seen as constituting the relation between the two realms, the answer must be given: that apart from the Church, nowhere is there any fundamental knowledge of the reasons which make the State legitimate and necessary. For everywhere else, save in the Church, the State, and every individual state, with its concern for human justice, may be called in question. From the point of view of the Church that preaches divine justification to all men this is impossible. For in the view of the Church, the authority of the State is included in the authority of their Lord Jesus Christ. The Church lives in expectation of the eternal State, and therefore honours the earthly State, and constantly expects the best from it, i.e., that, in its own way amongst "all men," it will serve the Lord whom the believers already love as their Saviour. For the sake of the freedom to preach justification, the Church expects that the State will be a true State, and thus that it will create and administer justice. But the Church honours the State even when this expectation is not fulfilled. It is then defending the State against the State, and by rendering unto God the things that are God's, by obeying God rather than man, through its intercession it represents the only possibility of restoring the State and of saving it from ruin. States may rise and fall, political conceptions may change, politics as such may interest or may fail to interest men, but throughout all developments and all changes *one* factor remains, as the preservation and basis of all states—the Christian Church. What do statesmen and politicians themselves know of the authorization and the necessity of their function? Who or what can give them the assurance that this function of theirs is not, as such, an illusion, however seriously they may take it? And further, what do those others know, whose responsibility for the State and its law the statesman alone can represent, and on whose co-operation they are finally so dependent! Just as divine justification is the continuum of law, so the Church is the political continuum. And to be this is the Church's first and fundamental service to the State. The Church need only be truly "Church," and it will inevitably render this service. And the State receives this service, and secretly lives by it, whether it knows and gratefully acknowledges it or not, whether it wishes to receive it or not.

We only *seem* to be moving in a lower sphere when, turning again to Romans 13:5–7, we note that the Church here demands from her members, with an insistence elsewhere unparalleled, the fulfilment of those *duties* on the performance of which not merely the goodness or the badness of the State but its very existence as a State depends. The fact that the right to impose rates and taxes belongs to the State, that its laws and their representatives should be honoured, as such, with all respect and reverence, can only be stated unreservedly and in a binding way from the standpoint of the divine justification of sinful man, because this provides the only protection against the sophisms and excuses of man, who is always so ready to justify himself and is always secretly trying to escape from true law. The Church knows that the State can neither establish nor protect true human law, *"ius unum et necessarium,"* that is, the law of freedom for the preaching of justification, unless it receives its due from the Church, whereby alone it can exist as guarantor of law—that is why the Church demands that this due should be rendered in all circumstances.

We would of course give a great deal to receive more specific instruction in Romans 13—and elsewhere in the New Testament—about what is and what is not to be understood by these particular political duties towards the State which are expected of the Church. The questions which arise in this connection cannot be answered directly

from the New Testament; all that we can do is to give re-
plies which are derived from the consideration of these passages by carrying the thought further along the same lines.
Could Romans 13:7, for instance, also mean "an oath to
whom an oath"? Does the rendering of an oath, if demanded by the State, belong to those duties that must be
fulfilled? The Reformers, as we know, answered this question in the affirmative, but on looking at Matthew 5:33 ff.,
we could wish that they had given a little more thought
to the matter. So much, at least, is certain, even if the question is answered in the affirmative, that an oath to the State
cannot be given (with true respect for the State!) if it is
a "totalitarian" oath (that is, if it is rendered to a name
which actually claims Divine functions). Such an oath
would indeed imply that those who swear it place themselves at the disposition of a power which threatens the freedom of the Word of God; for Christians, therefore, this
would mean the betrayal of the Church and of its Lord.

Again, is *military service* one of these self-evident duties
to the State? The Reformers again answered this question
in the affirmative, and again we could wish that they had
done so with a little more reserve. Because the State
"beareth the sword" (Romans 13), it is clear that it participates in the murderous nature of the present age. Yet on
this matter, at least in principle, we cannot come to a conclusion which differs from that of the Reformers. Human
law needs the guarantee of human force. Man would not
be a sinner in need of justification if it were otherwise. The
State that is threatened from within or without by force
needs to be prepared to meet force by force, if it is to continue to be a state. The Christian must have very real
grounds for distrusting the State if he is to be entitled to
refuse the State his service, and if the Church as such is
to be entitled and called to say "No" at this point. A fundamental Christian "No" cannot be given here, because it
would in fact be a fundamental "No" to the earthly State
as such, which is impossible from the Christian point of

view. And here I should like to add, in relation to the question of national defense in Switzerland in particular, that here, too, there can for us be no practical refusal of military service. We may have gra\ ⟩ misgivings about the way in which the Swiss State seeks to be a just state, but, all the same, we cannot maintain that it confronts the Church like "the Beast out of the abyss" of Revelation 13. But this may and should be said of more than one other State to-day, against which it is worthwhile to defend our own legal administration. And since this is the case, from the Christian point of view we are right in seeking to defend our frontiers; and if the State in Switzerland takes steps to organize this security (it is not inconceivable that the Church should give its support to the State in this matter), we cannot close our eyes to the question of how far the Church in Switzerland should stand in all surety behind the State.[33]

It is quite another question whether the State has any right to try to strengthen its authority by making any kind of *inward* claim upon its subjects and its citizens; that is, whether it has any right to demand from them a particular philosophy of life (Weltanschauung), or at least sentiments and reactions dominated by a particular view imposed by the State from without. According to the New Testament, the only answer to this question is an unhesitating "No"! Claims of this kind can in no way be inferred from Romans 13; they have no legal justification whatsoever. On the contrary, here we are very near the menace of "the Beast out of the abyss"; a just State will not require to make such claims. From Romans 13 it is quite clear that love is not one of the duties which we owe to the State. When the State begins to claim "love," it is in process of becoming a Church, the Church of a false God, and thus an unjust State. The just State requires, not love, but a simple, resolute, and responsible attitude on the part of its citizens. It

[33] It is obvious that the same is also true of the Church in Czechoslovakia, in Holland, in Denmark, in Scandinavia, in France and, above all, in England.

is this attitude which the Church, based on justification, commends to its members.

Far more difficult, because far more fundamental, is another apparent gap in the teaching of the New Testament. It lies in the fact that the New Testament seems to speak concretely only of a purely authoritarian State, and so to speak of Christians only as subjects, not as citizens who, in their own persons, bear some responsibility for the State. But it is to be hoped that the fulfilment of our political duty is not exhausted by the payment of taxes and other such passive forms of legality. For us the fulfilment of political duty means rather responsible choice of authority, responsible decision about the validity of laws, responsible care for their maintenance, in a word, political action, which may and must also mean political struggle. If the Church were not to guarantee the modern State the fulfilment of such duties, what would it have to offer the "democratic" State? Here, too, we must ask: are we following a legitimate line of expansion of the thought of Romans 13? It may seem audacious to answer that question in the affirmative, yet it must be firmly answered in the affirmative. Everything here depends on whether we are justified in this connection in taking the "be subject unto" of Romans 13 together with the exhortation to intercession in I Timothy 2. If the prayer of Christians for the State constitutes the norm of their "subjection," which would only be an "annexe" of the priestly function of the Church, and if this prayer is taken seriously as the responsible intercession of the Christians for the State, then the scheme of purely passive subjection which apparently—but only apparently—governs the thought of Romans 13 is broken. Then the serious question arises: is it an accident that in the course of time "democratic" States have come into being, States, that is, which are based upon the responsible activity of their citizens?[34]

[34] Under this category it is proper to include also such "monarchies" as those of England and Holland. The assertion that all forms of government are equally compatible or incompatible

Can serious prayer, in the long run, continue without the corresponding work? Can we ask God for something which we are not at the same moment determined and prepared to bring about, so far as it lies within the bounds of our possibility? Can we pray that the State shall preserve us, and that it may continue to do so as a just State, or that it will again become a just State, and not at the same time pledge ourselves personally, both in thought and action, in order that this may happen, without sharing the earnest desire of the Scottish Confession[35] and saying, with it: "*Vitae bonorum adesse, tyrranidem opprimere, ab infirmioribus vim improborum defendere*," thus without, in certain cases, like Zwingli,[36] reckoning with the possibility of revolution, the possibility, according to his strong expression, that we may have to "overthrow with God" those rulers who do not follow the lines laid down by Christ? Can we give the State that respect which is its due without making its business our own, with *all* the consequences that this implies? When I consider the deepest and most central content of the New Testament exhortation, I should say that we are justified, from the point of view of exegesis, in regarding the "democratic conception of the State" as a justifiable expansion of the thought of the New Testament. This does not mean that the separation between justification and justice, between Church and State, the fact that Christians are "foreigners" in the sphere of the State, has been abolished. On the contrary, the resolute intention of the teaching of the New Testament is brought out still more plainly when it is clear that Christians must not only endure the earthly State but that they must *will* it, and that they can-

---

with the Gospel is not only outworn but false. It is true that a man may go to hell in a democracy and achieve salvation under a mobocracy or a dictatorship. But it is not true that a Christian can endorse, desire, or seek after a mobocracy or a dictatorship as readily as a democracy.

[35] Art. 14.

[36] Schlussreden, Art. 42.

not will it as a "Pilate" State, but as a *just* State; when it is seen that there is no outward escape from the political sphere; when it is seen that Christians, while they remain within the Church and are wholly committed to the future "city," are equally committed to responsibility for the earthly "city," called to work and (it may be) to struggle, as well as to pray, for it; in short, when each one of them is responsible for the character of the State as a just State. And the democratic State might as well recognize that it can expect no truer or more complete fulfilment of duty than that of the citizens of the realm that is so foreign to it as a State—the Church founded on divine justification.

There is one last point to be discussed concerning the guarantee that the Church has to grant to the State. We remember how the New Testament exhortation to a certain extent culminates in the affirmation that Christians should render unto Caesar the things that are Caesar's by their well-doing. But what does this mean if by this "well-doing" we understand not a neutral moral goodness, but a life lived in faith in Jesus Christ, the life of the Children of God, the life of the Church as such? It then means that the essential service of the Church to the State simply consists in maintaining and occupying its own realm as Church. In so doing it will secure, in the best possible way, the position of the State, which is quite different. By proclaiming divine justification it will be rendering the best possible assistance to the establishment and maintenance of human justice and law. No direct action that the Church might take (acting partly or wholly politically, with well-meaning zeal) could even remotely be compared with the positive relevance of that action whereby, without any interference with the sphere of the State, this Church proclaims the coming Kingdom of Christ, and thereby the gospel of justification through faith alone; I mean that its action consists in true scriptural *preaching,* and *teaching,* and in the true and scriptural administration of the *sacraments.* When it performs this action the Church is, within the order of creation, the force which founds and maintains the State. If the State is wise, in the last resort it will expect and demand from the Church nothing other than this, for this includes everything that the Church can render to the State, even all the political obligations of its members. And we can and may formulate the matter even more precisely: the guarantee of the State by the Church is finally accomplished when the Church claims for itself the guarantee of the State, i.e., the guarantee of freedom to proclaim her message. This may sound strange, but this is the case: all that can be said from the standpoint of divine justification on the question (and the questions) of human law is summed up in this one statement: the Church *must have freedom to proclaim divine justification.* The State will realize its own potentialities, and thus will be a just State, in proportion as it not merely positively allows, but actively grants, this freedom to the Church; i.e., in proportion as it honourably and consistently desires to be the State within whose realm (whether as national Church or otherwise is a secondary question) the Church exists which has this freedom as its right. We know that the earthly State is neither called, nor able, to establish on earth the eternal law of the heavenly Jerusalem, because no human beings are either called, or able, to perform that task. But the State is called to establish human law, and it has the capacity to do so. We cannot measure what this law is by any Romantic or Liberalistic idea of "natural law," but simply by the concrete law of freedom, which the Church must claim for its Word, so far as it is the Word of God. This right of the Church to liberty means the foundation, the maintenance, the restoration of everything—certainly of all human law. Wherever this right is recognized, and wherever a true Church makes the right use of it (and the free preaching of justification will see to it that things fall into their true place), there we shall find a legitimate human authority and an equally legitimate human independence; tyranny on the one hand, and anarchy on the other, Fascism and Bolshevism alike,

will be dethroned; and the true order of human affairs—
the justice, wisdom and peace, equity and care for human
welfare which are necessary to that true order—will arise.
Not as heaven (not even as a miniature heaven) on earth!
No, this "true order" will be able to arise only upon this
earth and within the *present age*, but this will take place
really and *truly*, already upon this earth, and in this present
age, in this world of sin and sinners. No eternal Solomon,
free from temptation and without sin, but none the less a
Solomon, an image of Him whose Kingdom will be a Kingdom of Peace without frontiers and without end. This is
what the Church has to offer to the State when, on its side,
it desires from the State nothing but freedom. What more
could the State require, and what could be of greater service to it than this—to be taken so inexorably seriously?

We all know the maxim of Frederick the Great: *Suum
cuique.* It is a less well-known fact that it already appears
as a definition of human law, as a summary of the functions
of the just State, in Calvin's *Institutio: ut suum cuique
salvum sit et incolume.*[37] But—this Calvin did not say, and
this we must attempt to discover and to learn anew—it depends upon the justification of sinful man in Jesus Christ,
and thus on the maintenance of this central message of the
Christian Church, that all *this* should become true and valid
in every sense, in the midst of this "world that passeth
away," in the midst of the great, but temporary contrast
between Church and State, in the period which the Divine
patience has granted us between the resurrection of Jesus
Christ and His return: *Suum cuique.*

[37] Inst. IV., 20, 3. And, as was kindly pointed out to me by
Dr. Arnold Eberhard of Lörrach, there is no doubt that Calvin
was on his side quoting Ulpian and Cicero.

THE CHRISTIAN
COMMUNITY AND THE
CIVIL COMMUNITY

I

By the "Christian community" we mean what is usually called "the Church" and by the "civil community" what is usually called "the State."

The use of the concept of the "community" to describe both entities may serve at the very outset to underline the positive relationship and connexion between them. It was probably with some such intention in mind that Augustine spoke of the *civitas coelestis* and *terrena* and Zwingli of divine and human justice. In addition, however, the twofold use of the concept "community" is intended to draw attention to the fact that we are concerned in the "Church" and the "State" not merely and not primarily with institutions and offices but with human beings gathered together in corporate bodies in the service of common tasks. To interpret the "Church" as meaning above all a "community" has rightly become more recognised and normal again in recent years. The Swiss term "civil community"—in Swiss villages the residential, civil, and ecclesiastical communities often confer one after the other in the same inn, and most of the people involved belong to all three groups—the "civil community" as opposed to the "Christian community" may also remind Christians that there are and always have been communities outside their own circle in the form of States, i.e. political communities.

The "Christian community" (the Church) is the commonalty of the people in one place, region, or country who are called apart and gathered together as "Christians" by reason of their knowledge of and belief in Jesus Christ. The meaning and purpose of this "assembly" (*ekklesia*) is the common life of these people in one Spirit, the Holy Spirit, that is, in obedience to the Word of God in Jesus Christ, which they have all heard and are all needing and eager to hear again. They have also come together in order to pass on the Word to others. The inward expression of their life as a Christian community is the one faith, love, and hope by which they are all moved and sustained; its outward expression is the Confession by which they all stand, their jointly acknowledged and exercised responsibility for the preaching of the Name of Jesus Christ to all men and the worship and thanksgiving which they offer together. Since this is its concern, every single Christian community is as such an ecumenical (catholic) fellowship, that is, at one with the Christian communities in all other places, regions, and lands.

The "civil community" (the State) is the commonalty of all the people in one place, region, or country in so far as they belong together under a constitutional system of government that is equally valid for and binding on them all, and which is defended and maintained by force. The meaning and purpose of this mutual association (that is, of the *polis*) is the safeguarding of both the external, relative, and provisional freedom of the individuals and the external and relative peace of their community and to that extent the safeguarding of the external, relative, and provisional humanity of their life both as individuals and as a community. The three essential forms in which this safeguarding takes place are (a) legislation, which has to settle the legal system which is to be binding on all; (b) the government and administration which has to apply the legislation; (c) the administration of justice which has to deal with cases of doubtful or conflicting law and decide on its applicability.

II

When we compare the Christian community with the civil community the first difference that strikes us is that in the civil community Christians are no longer gathered together as such but are associated with non-Christians (or doubtful Christians). The civil community embraces everyone living within its area. Its members share no common awareness of their relationship to God, and such an awareness cannot be an element in the legal system established by the civil community. No appeal can be made to the Word or Spirit of God in the running of its affairs. The civil community as such is spiritually blind and ignorant. It has neither faith nor love nor hope. It has no creed and no gospel. Prayer is not part of its life, and its members are not brothers and sisters. As members of the civil community they can only ask, as Pilate asked: What is truth? Since every answer to the question abolishes the presuppositions of the very existence of the civil community. "Tolerance" is its ultimate wisdom in the "religious" sphere—"religion" being used in this context to describe the purpose of the Christian community. For this reason the civil community can only have external, relative, and provisional tasks and aims, and that is why it is burdened and defaced by something which the Christian community can, characteristically, do without: physical force, the "secular arm" which it can use to enforce its authority. That is why it lacks the ecumenical breadth and freedom that are so essential to Christianity. The *polis* has walls. Up till now, at least, civil communities have always been more or less clearly marked off from one another as local, regional, national, and therefore competing and colliding units of government. And that is why the State has no safeguard or corrective against the danger of either neglecting or absolutising itself and its particular system and thus in one way or the other destroying and annulling itself. One cannot in fact compare the Church with the State without realising how much weaker, poorer, and more exposed to danger the human community is in the State than in the Church.

III

It would be inadvisable, however, to make too much of the comparison. According to the fifth thesis of the *Theological Declaration* of Barmen (1934), the Christian community also exists in "the still unredeemed world," and there is not a single problem harassing the State by which the Church is not also affected in some way or other. From a distance it is impossible clearly to distinguish the Christian from the non-Christian, the real Christian from the doubtful Christian even in the Church itself. Did not Judas the traitor participate in the Last Supper? Awareness of God is one thing, Being in God quite another. The Word and Spirit of God are no more automatically available in the Church than they are in the State. The faith of the Church can become frigid and empty; its love can grow cold; its hope can fall to the ground; its message become timid and even silent; its worship and thanksgiving mere formalities; its fellowship may droop and decay.

Even the Church does not simply "have" faith or love or hope. There are dead churches, and unfortunately one does not have to look far to find them anywhere. And if, normally, the Church renounces the use of physical force and has not shed blood, sometimes the only reason has been lack of opportunity; struggles for power have never been entirely absent in the life of the Church. Again, side by side with other and more far-reaching centrifugal factors, local, regional, and national differences in the Church's way of life have been and still are strong. The centripetal forces which it needs are still weak enough to make even the unity of Christian communities among themselves extremely doubtful in many places and a special "ecumenical" movement both desirable and urgently necessary. There is then no cause for the Church to regard the civil community too superciliously.

IV

More important still, however, is the positive relationship between the two communities which results from the fact that the constitutive elements of the civil community are also proper and indispensable to the Christian community. The very term *ekklesia* is borrowed from the political sphere. The Christian community also lives and acts within the framework of an order of law which is binding on all its members, of a "canon law" which it cannot regard as an end in itself but which it cannot neglect to institute as a "token of the Lordship of Christ" (A. de Quervain, *Kirche, Volk und Staat*, 1945, p. 158). The Christian community exists at all times and places as a *politeia* with definite authorities and offices, with patterns of community life and divisions of labour. What the legislature, the executive, and the administration of the law are in the life of the State has its clear parallels in the life of the Church, however freely and flexibly it may be shaped and however "spiritually" it may be established and intended. And though the Christian community does not embrace all men, but only those who profess themselves Christians and would like, more or less seriously, to be Christians—it reaches out, instituted as it is to be the "light of the world," from these few or many, to all men. The gospel, with which it is commissioned, is preached to all, applies to all. To serve all the people within range of the place, region, or country where it is established is the purpose of its existence no less than it is that of the civil community. In I Timothy 2:1–7 we read that the God in whose sight it is good and acceptable that Christians as such may lead a quiet and peaceable life in all godliness and honesty will have all men to be saved and to come to the knowledge of the truth, and that Christians are therefore to pray for all men and especially for "kings," that is, for those who bear special responsibility in the political sphere (which embraces all men).

In this sense, therefore, the existence of the Christian community is political. Furthermore, the object of the promise and the hope in which the Christian community has its eternal goal consists, according to the unmistakable assertion of the New Testament, not in an eternal Church but in the *polis* built by God and coming down from heaven to earth, and the nations shall walk in the light of it and the kings of the earth will bring their glory and honour into it (Revelation 21:2, 24)—it consists in a heavenly *politeuma* (Philippians 3:20)—in the *basileia* of God—in the judgment of the King on the throne of His glory (Matthew 25:31 f.). Bearing all this in mind, we are entitled and compelled to regard the existence of the Christian community as of ultimate and supremely political significance.

V

The Christian community is particularly conscious of the need for the existence of the civil community. For it knows that all men (non-Christians as well as Christians) need to have "kings," that is, need to be subject to an external, relative, and provisional order of law, defended by superior authority and force. It knows that the original and final pattern of this order is the eternal Kingdom of God and the eternal righteousness of His grace. It preaches the Kingdom of God in this external form. But it also thanks God that His Kingdom has an external, relative, and provisional embodiment "in the world that is not yet redeemed," in which it is valid and effective even when the temporal order is based on the most imperfect and clouded knowledge of Jesus Christ or on no such knowledge at all. This external, relative, and provisional, but not on that account invalid or ineffective, form of legal order is the civil community. The Christian community is aware of the need for the civil community, and it alone takes the need absolutely seriously. For—because it knows of the Kingdom and grace of God—it knows of man's presumption and the plainly destructive consequences of man's presumption. It knows how dangerous man is and how endangered by himself. It knows him as a sinner, that is as a being who is always on the point of opening the sluices through which, if he were not checked in time, chaos and nothingness would break in and bring human time to an end. It can only conceive the time that is still left to it as a "time of grace" in the twofold sense of being the time which it is given in order to know and lay hold of God's grace—and as the time which it is given for this very purpose by the grace of God. The Christian community itself exists in this time which is given to man, that is, in the space where man's temporal life is still protected from chaos—and on the face of it chaos should have broken in long ago. It sees as the visible means of this protection of human life from chaos the existence of the civil community, the State's effort to achieve an external, relative, and provisional humanising of man's life and the political order instituted for all (for non-Christians as well as Christians—they both need it, for human arrogance is alive in both), under which the evil are punished and the good rewarded (Romans 13:3; I Peter 2:14) and which guarantees that the worst is prevented from happening. It knows that without this political order there would be no Christian order. It knows and it thanks God that—as the inner circle within the wider circle (cf. O. Cullmann, *Königscherrschaft Christi und Kirche im Neuen Testament*, 1941)—it is allowed to share the protection which the civil community affords.

VI

Knowing that, it recognises in the existence of the civil community—disregarding the Christianity or lack of Christianity of its members and officials and also disregarding the particular forms which it assumes—no less than in its own existence, the operation of a divine ordinance (*ordinatio*, i.e. institution or foundation), an *exousia* which is and acts in accordance with the will of God (Romans 13:1 f.). However much human error and human tyranny may be involved in it, the State is not a product of sin but one of the constants of the divine Providence and government of the world in its action against human sin: it is therefore an instrument of divine grace. The civil community shares both a common origin and a common centre with the Christian community. It is an order of divine grace inasmuch as in relation to sinful man as such, in relation to the world that still needs redeeming, the grace of God is always the patience of God. It is the sign that mankind, in its total ignorance and darkness, which is still, or has again become, a prey to sin and therefore subject to the wrath of God, is yet not forsaken but preserved and sustained by God. It serves to protect man from the invasion of chaos and therefore to give him time: time for the preaching of the gospel; time for repentance; time for faith. Since "according to the measure of human insight and human capacity" and "under the threat and exercise of force" (Barmen Thesis No. 5), provision is made in the State for the establishment of human law and (in the inevitably external, relative, and provisional sense) for freedom, peace, and humanity, it renders a definite service to the divine Providence and plan of salvation, quite apart from the judgment and individual desires of its members. Its existence is not separate from the Kingdom of Jesus Christ; its foundations and its influence are not autonomous. It is outside the Church but not outside the range of Christ's dominion—it is an exponent of His Kingdom. It is, according to the New Testament, one of the "powers" created through Him and in Him and which subsist in Him (Colossians 1:16 f.), which cannot separate us from the love of God (Romans 8:37 f.) because they are all given to Him and are at His disposal (Matthew 28:18).

The activity of the State is, as the Apostle explicitly stated (Romans 13:4, 6), a form of divine service. As such it can be perverted just as the divine service of the Church itself is not exempt from the possibility of perversion. The State can assume the face and character of Pilate. Even then, however, it still acts in the power which God has given it ("Thou couldest have no power at all against me, except it were given thee from above": John 19:11). Even in its perversion it cannot escape from God; and His law is the standard by which it is judged. The Christian community therefore acknowledges "the benefaction of this ordinance of His with thankful, reverent hearts" (Barmen Thesis No. 5). The benefaction which it acknowledges consists in the external, relative, and provisional sanctification of the unhallowed world which is brought about by the existence of political power and order. In what concrete attitudes to particular political patterns and realities this Christian acknowledgement will be expressed can remain a completely open question. It makes one thing quite impossible, however: a Christian decision to be indifferent; a non-political Christianity. The Church can in no case be indifferent or neutral towards this manifestation of an order so clearly related to its own mission. Such indifference would be equivalent to the opposition of which it is said in Romans 13:2 that it is a rebellion against the ordinance of God—and rebels secure their own condemnation.

VII

The Church must remain the Church. It must remain the inner circle of the Kingdom of Christ. The Christian community has a task of which the civil community can never relieve it and which it can never pursue in the forms peculiar to the civil community. It would not redound to the welfare of the civil community if the Christian community were to be absorbed by it (as Rothe has suggested that it should) and were therefore to neglect the special task which it has received a categorical order to undertake. It proclaims the rule of Jesus Christ and the hope of the Kingdom of God. This is not the task of the civil community; it has no message to deliver; it is dependent on a message being delivered to it. It is not in a position to appeal to the authority and grace of God; it is dependent on this happening elsewhere. It does not pray; it depends on others praying for it. It is blind to the whence and whither of human existence; its task is rather to provide for the external and provisional delimitation and protection of human life; it depends on the existence of seeing eyes elsewhere. It cannot call the human *hybris* into question fundamentally, and it knows of no final defence against the chaos which threatens it from that quarter; in this respect, too, it depends on ultimate words and insights existing elsewhere. The thought and speech of the civil community waver necessarily between a much too childlike optimism and a much too peevish pessimism in regard to man—as a matter of course it expects the best of everybody and suspects the worst! It obviously relies on its own view of man being fundamentally superseded elsewhere. Only an act of supreme disobedience on the part of Christians could bring the special existence of the Christian community to an end. Such a cessation is also impossible because then the voice of what is ultimately the only hope and help which all men need to hear would be silent.

VIII

The Christian community shares in the task of the civil community precisely to the extent that it fulfils its own task. By believing in Jesus Christ and preaching Jesus Christ it believes in and preaches Him who is Lord of the world as He is Lord of the Church. And since they belong to the inner circle, the members of the Church are also automatically members of the wider circle. They cannot halt at the boundary where the inner and outer circles meet, though the work of faith, love, and hope which they are under orders to perform will assume different forms on either side of the boundary. In the sphere of the civil community the Christian community shares common interests with the world and its task is to give resolute practical expression to this community of interest. The Christian community prays for the civil community. It does so all the more since the civil community as such is not in the habit of praying. But by praying for it, it also makes itself responsible for it before God, and it would not be taking this responsibility seriously if it did no more than pray, if it did not also work actively on behalf of the civil community. It also expresses its active support of the civil community by acknowledging that, as an operation of a divine ordinance, the civil power is also binding on Christians and significant and just from the Christian point of view. It expresses its active support of the civil community by "subordinating" itself, in the words of the Apostle (Romans 13:1), to the cause of the civil community under all circumstances (and therefore whatever the political form and reality it has to deal with *in concreto*). Luther's translation speaks of "being *subject*" (cf. English A.V.: "Let every soul be *subject* to the higher powers"—Trans.), which is something dangerously different from what is meant here. The last thing this instruction implies is that the Christian community and the Christian should offer the blindest possible obedience to the civil community and its officials. What is meant is (Romans 13:6 f.) that Christians should carry out what is required of them for the establishment, preservation, and maintenance of the civil community and for the execution of its task, because, although they are Christians and, as such, have their home elsewhere, they also live in this outer circle. Jesus Christ is still its centre: they, too, are therefore responsible for its stability. "Subordination" means the carrying out of this joint responsibility in which Christians apply themselves to the same task with non-Christians and submit themselves to the same rule. The subordination accrues to the good of the civil community however well or however badly that community is defended, because the civil cause (and not merely the Christian cause) is also the cause of the one God. In Romans 13:5 Paul has expressly added that this "subordination" is not optional but necessary, and necessary not merely "for fear of punishment," for fear of the otherwise inevitable conflict with an obscure commandment of God, but "for conscience sake": in the clear evangelical knowledge of the divine grace and patience, which is also manifested in the existence of the State and, therefore, in full responsibility towards the will of God which the Christian sees revealed in the civil community. The "subordination" will be an expression of the obedience of a free heart which the Christian offers to God in the civil sphere as in the sphere of the Church—although with a different purpose (he renders to Caesar what is Caesar's and to God what is God's—Matthew 22:21).

IX

In making itself jointly responsible for the civil community, the Christian community has no exclusive theory of its own to advocate in face of the various forms and realities of political life. It is not in a position to establish one particular doctrine as *the* Christian doctrine of the just State. It is also not in a position to refer to any past realisation of the perfect State or to hold out any prospect of one in the future. There is but one Body of Christ, born of the Word of God, which is heard in faith. There is therefore no such thing as a Christian State corresponding to the Christian Church; there is no duplicate of the Church in the political sphere. For if, as the effect of a divine ordinance, as the manifestation of one of the constants of divine Providence and of the historical process which it governs, the State is in the Kingdom of Christ, this does not mean that God is revealed, believed, and perceived in any political community as such. The effect of the divine ordinance is that men are entrusted (whether or not they believe it to be a divine revelation) to provide "according to the measure of human insight and human capacity" for temporal law and temporal peace, for an external, relative, and provisional humanisation of man's existence. Accordingly, the various political forms and systems are human inventions which as such do not bear the distinctive mark of revelation and are not witnessed to as such—and can therefore not lay any claim to belief. By making itself jointly responsible for the civil community, the Christian community participates—on the basis of and by belief in the divine revelation—in the human search for the best form, for the most fitting system of political organisation; but it is also aware of the limits of all the political forms and systems which man can discover (even with the co-operation of the Church), and it will beware of playing off one political concept—even the "democratic" concept—as *the* Christian concept, against all others. Since it proclaims the Kingdom of God it has to maintain its own hopes and questions in the face of all purely political concepts. And this applies even more to all political achievements. Though the Christian will be both more lenient and more stern, more patient and more impatient towards them than the non-Christian, he will not regard any such achievement as perfect or mistake it for the Kingdom of God—for it can only have been brought about by human insight and human ability. In the face of all political achievements, past, present, and future, the Church waits for "the city which hath foundations, whose builder and maker is God" (Hebrews 11:10). It trusts and obeys no political system or reality but the power of the Word, by which God upholds all things (Hebrews 1:3; Barmen Thesis No. 5), including all political things.

X

In this freedom, however, the Church makes itself responsible for the shape and reality of the civil community in a quite definite sense. We have already said that it is quite impossible for the Christian to adopt an attitude of complete indifference to politics. But neither can the Church be indifferent to particular political patterns and realities. The Church "reminds the world of God's Kingdom, God's commandment and righteousness and thereby of the responsibility of governments and governed" (Barmen Thesis No. 5). This means that the Christian community and the individual Christian can understand and accept many things in the political sphere—and if necessary suffer and endure everything. But the fact that it can understand much and endure everything has nothing to do with the "subordination" which is required of it, that is, with the share of responsibility which it is enjoined to take in the political sphere. That responsibility refers rather to the decisions which it must make before God: "must" make, because, unlike Christian understanding and suffering, Christian intentions and decisions are bound to run in a quite definite direction of their own. There will always be room and need for discussion on the details of Christian intentions and decisions, but the general line on which they are based can never be the subject of accommodation and compromise in the Church's relations with the world. The Christian community "subordinates" itself to the civil community by making its knowledge of the Lord who is Lord of all its criterion, and distinguishing between the just and the unjust State, that is, between the better and the worse political form and reality; between order and caprice; between government and tyranny; between freedom and anarchy; between community and collectivism; between personal rights and individualism; between the State as described in Romans 13 and the State as described in Revelation 13. And it will judge all matters concerned with the establishment, preservation, and enforcement of political order in accordance with these necessary distinctions and according to the merits of the particular case and situation to which they refer. On the basis of the judgment which it has formed it will choose and desire whichever seems to be the better political system in any particular situation, and in accordance with this choice and desire it will offer its support here and its resistance there. It is in the making of such distinctions, judgments, and choices from its own centre, and in the practical decisions which necessarily flow from that centre, that the Christian community expresses its "subordination" to the civil community and fulfils its share of political responsibility.

XI

The Christian decisions which have to be made in the political sphere have no idea, system, or programme to refer to but a direction and a line that must be recognised and adhered to in all circumstances. This line cannot be defined by appealing to the so-called "natural law." To base its policy on "natural law" would mean that the Christian community was adopting the ways of the civil community, which does not take its bearings from the Christian centre and is still living or again living in a state of ignorance. The Christian community would be adopting the methods, in other words, of the pagan State. It would not be acting as a Christian community in the State at all; it would no longer be the salt and the light of the wider circle of which Christ is the centre. It would not only be declaring its solidarity with the civil community: it would be putting itself on a par with it and withholding from it the very things it lacks most. It would certainly not be doing it any service in that way. For the thing the civil community lacks (in its neutrality towards the Word and Spirit of God) is a firmer and clearer motivation for political decisions than the so-called natural law can provide. By "natural law" we mean the embodiment of what man is alleged to regard as universally right and wrong, as necessary, permissible, and forbidden "by nature," that is, on any conceivable premise. It has been connected with a natural revelation of God, that is, with a revelation known to man by natural means. And the civil community as such—the civil community which is not yet or is no longer illuminated from its centre —undoubtedly has no other choice but to think, speak, and act on the basis of this allegedly natural law, or rather of a particular conception of the court of appeal which is passed off as *the* natural law. The civil community is reduced to guessing or to accepting some powerful assertion of this or that interpretation of natural law. All it can do is to grope around and experiment with the convictions which it derives from "natural law," never certain whether it may not in the end be an illusion to rely on it as the final authority and therefore always making vigorous use, openly or secretly, of a more or less refined positivism. The results of the politics based on such considerations were and are just what might be expected. And if they were and are not clearly and generally negative, if in the political sphere the better stands alongside the worse, if there were and still are good as well as bad States—no doubt the reality is always a curious mixture of the two!—then the reason is not that the true "natural law" has been discovered, but simply the fact that even the ignorant, neutral, pagan civil community is still in the Kingdom of Christ, and that all political questions and all political efforts as such are founded on the gracious ordinance of God by which man is preserved and his sin and crime confined.

What we glimpse in the better kind of State is the purpose, meaning, and goal of this divine ordinance. It is operative in any case, even though the citizens of the particular State may lack any certain knowledge of the trustworthy standards of political decision, and the overwhelming threat of mistaking an error for the truth may be close at hand. The divine ordinance may operate with the co-operation of the men and women involved, but certainly without their having deserved it: *Dei providentia hominum confusione.* If the Christian community were to base its political responsibility on the assumption that it was also interested in the problem of natural law and that it was attempting to base its decisions on so-called natural law, this would not alter the power which God has to make good come of evil, as He is in fact always doing in the political order. But it would mean that the Christian community was sharing human illusions and confusions. It is bad enough that, when it does not risk going its own way, the Christian community is widely involved in these illusions and confusions. It should not wantonly attempt to deepen such involvement. And it would be doing no less if it were to seek the criterion of its political decisions in some form of the so-called natural law. The tasks and problems which the Christian community is called to share, in fulfilment of its political responsibility, are "natural," secular, profane tasks and problems. But the norm by which it should be guided is anything but natural: it is the only norm which it can believe in and accept as a spiritual norm, and is derived from the clear law of its own faith, not from the obscure workings of a system outside itself: it is from knowledge of this norm that it will make its decisions in the political sphere.

XII

It is this reliance on a spiritual norm that makes the Christian community free to support the cause of the civil community honestly and calmly. In the political sphere the Church will not be fighting for itself and its own concerns. Its own position, influence, and power in the State are not the goal which will determine the trend of its political decisions. "My Kingdom is not of this world. If my Kingdom were of this world, then would my servants fight that I should not be delivered to the Jews, but now is my Kingdom not from hence" (John 18:36). The secret contempt which a Church fighting for its own interests with political weapons usually incurs even when it achieves a certain amount of success is well deserved. And sooner or later the struggle generally ends in mortifying defeats of one sort or another. The Christian community is not an end in itself. It serves God and it thereby serves man. It is true that the deepest, ultimate, divine purpose of the civil community consists in creating opportunities for the preaching and hearing of the Word and, to that extent, for the existence of the Church. But the only way the State can create such opportunities, according to the providence and ordinance of God, is the natural, secular, and profane way of the establishment of law, the safeguarding of freedom and peace, "according to the measure of human insight and capacity." The divine purpose is therefore not at all that the State should itself gradually develop more or less into a Church. And the Church's political aim cannot be to turn the State into a Church, that is, make it as far as possible subservient to the tasks of the Church. If the State grants the Church freedom, respect, and special privileges in any of the ways which are open to it (guarantees of one kind or another, a share in education and broadcasting, the defence of the Sabbath, financial reliefs or subsidies, and the like), the Church will not immediately start dreaming of a Church-State. It will be thankful for the State's help, seeing in such help a result of the divine providence and ordinance: and it will show its gratitude by being a Church all the more faithfully and zealously within the broader frontiers that the State's gifts make possible, thereby justifying the expectation which the State evidently reposes in it. But it will not claim such gifts as a right. If they are refused, it will look in itself for the reason, not in the State. "Resist not evil!" is an injunction that applies here. The Church will ask itself whether it has already given proof to the State of the Spirit and the power of God, whether it has already defended and proclaimed Jesus Christ to the world to the extent that it can expect to be considered an important, significant, and salutary factor in public life. It will ask, for example, whether it is in a position to say the tremendous things that are certainly entitled to be heard in schools. It will first and foremost do penance—when and where would it not have cause for so doing?—and it will do that best by concentrating on its own special work in the, possibly, extremely small space left to it in public life, with all the more confidence and intensity and with redoubled zeal, "with the greatest force applied at the narrowest point." Where it has first to advertise its desire to play a part in public life, where it must first establish its claim to be considered a factor of public importance, it only proves that its claim to be heard is irrelevant and it thoroughly deserves not to be heard at all, or to be heard in a way that will sooner or later afford it no pleasure. Whenever the Church has entered the political arena to fight for its claim to be given public recognition, it has always been a Church which has failed to understand the special purpose of the State, an impenitent, spiritually unfree Church.

XIII

The Church cannot, however, simply take the Kingdom of God itself into the political arena. The Church reminds men of God's Kingdom. This does not mean that it expects the State gradually to become the Kingdom of God. The Kingdom of God is the Kingdom where God is without shadow, without problems and contradictions, where He is All in All: it is the rule of God in the redeemed world. In the Kingdom of God the outward is annulled by the inward, the relative by the absolute, the provisional by the final. In the Kingdom of God there is no legislature, no executive, no legal administration. For in the Kingdom of God there is no sin to be reproved, no chaos to be feared and checked. The Kingdom of God is the world dominion of Jesus Christ in honour of the Father, revealed in the clear light of day. The State as such, the neutral, pagan, ignorant State knows nothing of the Kingdom of God. It knows at best of the various ideals based on natural law. The Christian community within the State does know about the Kingdom of God, however, and it brings it to man's attention. It reminds men of the Jesus Christ who came and is to come again. But it cannot do this by projecting, proposing, and attempting to enforce a State in the likeness of the Kingdom of God. The State is quite justified if it refuses to countenance all such Christian demands. It belongs to the very nature of the State that it is not and cannot become the Kingdom of God. It is based on an ordinance of God which is intended for the "world not yet redeemed" in which sin and the danger of chaos have to be taken into account with the utmost seriousness and in which the rule of Jesus Christ, though in fact already established, is still hidden. The State would be disavowing its own purpose if it were to act as though its task was to become the Kingdom of God. And the Church that tried to induce it to develop into the Kingdom of God could be rightly reproached for being much too rashly presumptuous. If its demand were to have any meaning at all, it would have to believe that its own duty was also to develop into the Kingdom of God. But, like the State, the Church also stands "in the world not yet redeemed." And even at its best the Church is not an image of the Kingdom of God. It would appear that when it makes this demand on the State, the Church has also confused the Kingdom of God with a mere ideal of the natural law. Such a Church needs to be reminded again of the real Kingdom of God, which will follow both State and Church in time. A free Church will not allow itself to be caught on this path.

XIV

The direction of Christian judgments, purposes, and ideals in political affairs is based on the analogical capacities and needs of political organisation. Political organisation can be neither a repetition of the Church nor an anticipation of the Kingdom of God. In relation to the Church it is an independent reality; in relation to the Kingdom of God it is (like the Church itself) a human reality bearing the stamp of this fleeting world. An equating of State and

Church on the one hand and State and Kingdom of God on the other is therefore out of the question. On the other hand, however, since the State is based on a particular divine ordinance, since it belongs to the Kingdom of God, it has no autonomy, no independence over against the Church and the Kingdom of God. A simple and absolute heterogeneity between State and Church on the one hand and State and Kingdom of God on the other is therefore just as much out of the question as a simple and absolute equating. The only possibility that remains—and it suggests itself compellingly—is to regard the existence of the State as an allegory, as a correspondence and an analogue to the Kingdom of God which the Church preaches and believes in. Since the State forms the outer circle, within which the Church, with the mystery of its faith and gospel, is the inner circle, since it shares a common centre with the Church, it is inevitable that, although its presuppositions and its tasks are its own and different, it is nevertheless capable of reflecting indirectly the truth and reality which constitute the Christian community. Since, however, the peculiarity and difference of its presuppositions and tasks and its existence as an outer circle must remain as they are, its justice and even its very existence as a reflected image of the Christian truth and reality cannot be given once and for all and as a matter of course but are, on the contrary, exposed to the utmost danger; it will always be questionable whether and how far it will fulfil its just purposes. To be saved from degeneration and decay it needs to be reminded of the righteousness which is a reflection of Christian truth. Again and again it needs a historical setting whose goal and content are the moulding of the State into an allegory of the Kingdom of God and the fulfilment of its righteousness. Human initiative in such situations cannot proceed from the State itself. As a purely civil community, the State is ignorant of the mystery of the Kingdom of God, the mystery of its own centre, and it is indifferent to the faith and gospel of the Christian community. As a civil community it can only draw from the porous wells of the so-called natural law. It cannot remind itself of the true criterion of its own righteousness, it cannot move towards the fulfilment of that righteousness in its own strength. It needs the wholesomely disturbing presence, the activity that revolves directly around the common centre, the participation of the Christian community in the execution of political responsibility. The Church is not the Kingdom of God, but it has knowledge of it; it hopes for it; it believes in it; it prays in the name of Jesus Christ, and it preaches His Name as the Name above all others. The Church is not neutral on this ground, and it is therefore not powerless. If it achieves only the great and necessary *metabasis eis allo genos* which is the share of political responsibility which it is enjoined to assume, then it will not be able to be neutral and powerless and deny its Lord in the other *genos*. If the Church takes up its share of political responsibility, it must mean that it is taking that human initiative which the State cannot take: it is giving the State the impulse which it cannot give itself; it is reminding the State of those things of which it is unable to remind itself. The distinctions, judgments, and choices which it makes in the political sphere are always intended to foster the illumination of the State's connexion with the order of divine salvation and grace and to discourage all the attempts to hide this connexion. Among the political possibilities open at any particular moment it will choose those which most suggest a correspondence to, an analogy and a reflection of, the content of its own faith and gospel.

In the decisions of the State, the Church will always support the side which clarifies rather than obscures the Lordship of Jesus Christ over the whole, which includes this political sphere outside the Church. The Church desires that the shape and reality of the State in this fleeting world should point towards the Kingdom of God, not away from it. Its desire is not that human politics should cross the politics of God, but that they should proceed, however distantly, on parallel lines.

It desires that the active grace of God, as revealed from heaven, should be reflected in the earthly material of the external, relative, and provisional actions and modes of action of the political community. It therefore makes itself responsible in the first and last place to God—the one God whose grace is revealed in Jesus Christ—by making itself responsible for the cause of the State. And so, with its political judgments and choices, it bears an implicit, indirect, but none the less real witness to the gospel.

Even its political activity is therefore a profession of its Christian faith. By its political activity it calls the State from neutrality, ignorance, and paganism into co-responsibility before God, thereby remaining faithful to its own particular mission. It sets in motion the historical process whose aim and content are the moulding of the State into the likeness of the Kingdom of God and hence the fulfilment of the State's own righteous purposes.

XV

The Church is based on the knowledge of the one eternal God, who as such became man and thereby proved Himself a neighbor to man, by treating him with compassion (Luke 10:36 f.). The inevitable consequence is that in the political sphere the Church will always and in all circumstances be interested primarily in human beings and not in some abstract cause or other, whether it be anonymous capital or the State as such (the functioning of its departments!) or the honour of the nation or the progress of civilisation or culture or the idea, however conceived, of the historical development of the human race. It will not be interested in this last idea even if "progress" is interpreted as meaning the welfare of future generations, for the attainment of which man, human dignity, human life in the present age are to be trampled underfoot. Right itself becomes wrong (*summum ius summa iniuria*) when it is allowed to rule as an abstract form, instead of serving the limitation and hence the preservation of man. The Church is at all times and in all circumstances the enemy of the idol Juggernaut. Since God Himself became man, man is the measure of all things, and man can and must only be used and, in certain circumstances, sacrificed, for man. Even the most wretched man—not man's egoism, but man's humanity—must be resolutely defended against the autocracy of every mere "cause." Man has not to serve causes; causes have to serve man.

XVI

The Church is witness of the divine justification, that is, of the act in which God in Jesus Christ established and confirmed His original claim to man and hence man's claim against sin and death. The future for which the Church waits is the definitive revelation of this divine justification. This means that the Church will always be found where the order of the State is based on a commonly acknowledged law, from submission to which no one is exempt, and which also provides equal protection for all. The Church will be found where all political activity is in all circumstances regulated by this law. The Church always stands for the constitutional State, for the maximum validity and application of that twofold rule (no exemption from and full protection by the law), and therefore it will always be against any degeneration of the constitutional State into tyranny or anarchy. The Church will never be found on the side of anarchy or tyranny. In its politics it will always be urging the civil community to treat this fundamental purpose of its existence with the utmost seriousness: the limiting and the preserving of man by the quest for and the establishment of law.

XVII

The Church is witness of the fact that the Son of man came to seek and to save the lost. And this implies that—casting all false impartiality aside—the Church must concentrate first on the lower and lowest levels of human society. The poor, the socially and economically weak and threatened, will always be the object of its primary and particular concern, and it will always insist on the State's special responsibility for these weaker members of society. That it will bestow its love on them, within the framework of its own task (as part of its service), is one thing and the most important thing; but it must not concentrate on this and neglect the other thing to which it is committed by its political responsibility: the effort to achieve such a fashioning of the law as will make it impossible for "equality before the law" to become a cloak under which strong and weak, independent and dependent, rich and poor, employers and employees, in fact receive different treatment at its hands: the weak being unduly restricted, the strong unduly protected. The Church must stand for social justice in the political sphere. And in choosing between the various socialistic possibilities (social-liberalism? co-operativism? syndicalism? free trade? moderate or radical Marxism?) it will always choose the movement from which it can expect the greatest measure of social justice (leaving all other considerations on one side).

XVIII

The Church is the fellowship of those who are freely called by the Word of grace and the Spirit and love of God to be the children of God. Translated into political terms, this means that the Church affirms, as the basic right which every citizen must be guaranteed by the State, the freedom to carry out his decisions in the politically lawful sphere, according to his own insight and choice, and therefore independently, and the freedom to live in certain spheres (the family, education, art, science, religion, culture), safeguarded but not regulated by law. The Church will not in all circumstances withdraw from and oppose what may be practically a dictatorship, that is, a partial and temporary limitation of these freedoms, but it will certainly withdraw from and oppose any out-and-out dictatorship such as the totalitarian State. The adult Christian can only wish to be an adult citizen, and he can only want his fellow citizens to live as adult human beings.

XIX

The Church is the fellowship of those who, as members of the one Body of the one Head, are bound and committed to this Lord of theirs and therefore to no other. It follows that the Church will never understand and interpret political freedom and the basic law which the State must guarantee to the individual citizen other than in the sense of the basic duty of responsibility which is required of him. (This was never made particularly clear in the classic proclamations of so-called "human rights" in America and France.) The citizen is responsible in the whole sphere of his freedom, political and non-political alike. And the civil community is naturally responsible in the maintenance of its freedom as a whole. Thus the Christian approach surpasses both individualism and collectivism. The Church knows and recognises the "interest" of the individual and of the "whole," but it resists them both when they want to have the last word. It subordinates them to the being of the citizen, the being of the civil community before the law, over which neither the individuals nor the "whole" are to hold sway, but which they are to seek after, to find, and to serve —always with a view to limiting and preserving the life of man.

XX

As the fellowship of those who live in one faith under one Lord on the basis of a Baptism in one Spirit, the Church must and will stand for the equality of the freedom and responsibility of all adult citizens, in spite of its sober insight into the variety of human needs, abilities, and tasks. It will stand for their equality before the law that unites and binds them all, for their equality in working together to establish and carry out the law, and for their equality in the limitation and preservation of human life that it secures. If, in accordance with a specifically Christian insight, it lies in the very nature of the State that this equality must not be restricted by any differences of religious belief or unbelief, it is all the more important for the Church to urge that the restriction of the political freedom and responsibility not only of certain classes and races but, supremely, of that of women is an arbitrary convention which does not deserve to be preserved any longer. If Christians are to be consistent there can be only one possible decision in this matter.

XXI

Since the Church is aware of the variety of the gifts and tasks of the one Holy Spirit in its own sphere, it will be alert and open in the political sphere to the need to separate the different functions and "powers"—the legislative, executive, and judicial—inasmuch as those who carry out any one of these functions should not carry out the others simultaneously. No human being is a god able to unite in his own person the functions of the legislator and the ruler, the ruler and the judge, without endangering the sovereignty of the law. The "people" is no more such a god than the Church is its own master and in sole possession of its powers. The fact is that within the community of the one people (by the people and for the people) definite and different services are to be performed by different persons, which, if they were united in one human hand, would disrupt rather than promote the unity of the common enterprise. With its awareness of the necessity that must be observed in this matter, the Church will give a lead to the State.

XXII

The Church lives from the disclosure of the true God and His revelation, from Him as the Light that has been lit in Jesus Christ to destroy the works of darkness. It lives in the dawning of the day of the Lord and its task in relation to the world is to rouse it and tell it that this day has dawned. The inevitable political corollary of this is that the Church is the sworn enemy of all secret policies and secret diplomacy. It is just as true of the political sphere as of any other that only evil can want to be kept secret. The distinguishing mark of the good is that it presses forward to the light of day. Where freedom and responsibility in the service of the State are one, whatever is said and done must be said and done before the ears and eyes of all, and the legislator, the ruler, and the judge can and must be ready to answer openly for all their actions—without thereby being necessarily dependent on the public or allowing themselves to be flurried. The statecraft that wraps itself up in darkness is the craft of a State which, because it is anarchic or tyrannical, is forced to hide the bad conscience of its citizens or officials. The Church will not on any account lend its support to that kind of State.

XXIII

The Church sees itself established and nourished by the free Word of God—the Word which proves its freedom in the Holy Scriptures at all times. And in its own sphere the Church believes that the human word is capable of being the free vehicle and mouthpiece of this free Word of God.

By a process of analogy, it has to risk attributing a positive and constructive meaning to the free human word in the political sphere. If it trusts the word of man in one sphere it cannot mistrust it on principle in the other. It will believe that human words are not bound to be empty or useless or even dangerous, but that the right words can clarify and control great decisions. At the risk of providing opportunities for empty, useless, and dangerous words to be heard, it will therefore do all it can to see that there is at any rate no lack of opportunity for the *right* word to be heard. It will do all it can to see that there are opportunities for mutual discussion in the civil community as the basis of common endeavours. And it will try to see that such discussion takes place openly. With all its strength it will be on the side of those who refuse to have anything to do with the regimentation, controlling, and censoring of public opinion. It knows of no pretext which would make that a good thing and no situation in which it could be necessary.

XXIV

As disciples of Christ, the members of His Church do not rule: they serve. In the political community, therefore, the Church can only regard all ruling that is not primarily a form of service as a diseased and never as a normal condition. No State can exist without the sanction of power. But the power of the good State differs from that of the bad State as *potestas* differs from *potentia*. *Potestas* is the power that follows and serves the law; *potentia* is the power that precedes the law, that masters and bends and breaks the law—it is the naked power which is directly evil. Bismarck— not to mention Hitler—was (in spite of the *Daily Bible Readings* on his bedside table) no model statesman because he wanted to establish and develop his work on naked power. The ultimate result of this all-too-consistently pursued aim was inevitable: "all that draw the sword shall perish by the sword." Christian political theory leads us in the very opposite direction.

XXV

Since the Church is ecumenical (catholic) by virtue of its very origin, it resists all abstract local, regional, and national interests in the political sphere. It will always seek to serve the best interests of the particular city or place where it is stationed. But it will never do this without at the same time looking out beyond the city walls. It will be conscious of the superficiality, relativity, and temporariness of the immediate city boundaries, and on principle it will always stand for understanding and cooperation within the wider circle. The Church will be the last to lend its support to mere parochial politics. *Pacta sunt servanda? Pacta sunt concludenda!* All cities of the realm must agree if their common cause is to enjoy stability and not fall to pieces. In the Church we have tasted the air of freedom and must bring others to taste it, too.

XXVI

The Church knows God's anger and judgment, but it also knows that His anger lasts but for a moment, whereas His mercy is for eternity. The political analogy of this truth is that violent solutions of conflicts in the political community —from police measures to law court decisions, from the armed rising against a regime that is no longer worthy of or equal to its task (in the sense of a revolt undertaken not to undermine but to restore the lawful authority of the State) to the defensive war against an external threat to the lawful State—must be approved, supported, and if necessary even suggested by the Christian community—for how could it possibly contract out in such situations? On the other hand, it can only regard violent solutions of any conflict as an *ultima ratio regis.* It will approve and support them only when they are for the moment the ultimate and only possibility available. It will always do its utmost to postpone such moments as far as possible. It can never stand for absolute peace, for peace at any price. But it must and will do all it can to see that no price is considered too high for the preservation or restoration of peace at home and abroad except the ultimate price which would mean the abolition of the lawful State and the practical denial of the divine ordinance. May the Church show her inventiveness in the search for other solutions before she joins in the call for violence! The perfection of the Father in heaven, who does not cease to be the heavenly Judge, demands the earthly perfection of a peace policy which really does extend to the limits of the humanly possible.

XXVII

These are a few examples of Christian choices, decisions, and activities in the political sphere: examples of analogies and corollaries of that Kingdom of God in which the Church believes and which it preaches, in the sphere of the external, relative, and provisional problems of the civil community. The translation of the Kingdom of God into political terms demands Christian, spiritual, and prophetic knowledge on every side. The points of comparison and the decisions we have quoted are in no sense equivalent to the paragraphs of a political constitution. They are merely intended to illustrate how the Church can make decisions on a Christian basis in the political sphere. We might have taken twice or three times as many or only half as many examples or just one example to make the vital point clear. We used examples because we were concerned to illuminate the analogical but extremely concrete relationship between the Christian gospel and certain political decisions and modes of behaviour. The only more concrete way of discussing the relationship would be to refer to individual historical decisions. The reason why we mentioned many examples was that we wanted to demonstrate that the essence of Christian politics is not a system or a succession of momentary brain waves but a constant direction, a continuous line of discoveries on both sides of the boundary which separates the political from the spiritual spheres, a correlation between explication and application. The list of such explications and applications that we have offered here is naturally incomplete. And it is of the very nature of all such points of contact and decision as have been or could have been mentioned that the translations and transitions from the one sphere to the other will always be open to discussion as far as the details are concerned, will only be more or less obvious and never subject to absolute proof. What we have said here needs to be extended, deepened, and particularised. The more one studies the problems of translation from one sphere to the other, the more one will realise that it is not possible to deal with every problem in this way. But the clarity of the message of the Bible will guarantee that all the explications and applications of the Christian approach will move in one unswerving direction and one continuous line. What we were concerned to show was the possibility and the necessity of comparisons and analogies between the two spheres and of the decisions which have to be made in the transition from one to the other.

XXVIII

Let me add a comment on the constancy and continuousness of the line of Christian political thought and action that we have indicated. We have argued not from any conception of "natural law" but from the gospel. It cannot be denied, however, that in the list of examples quoted we have more than once made assertions which have been justified elsewhere on the basis of natural law. We bear no grudge against anyone who may have been reminded of Rousseau —and who may have been pleased or angry on that account. We need not be ashamed of the affinity. We have seen that the divine ordinance of the State makes it perfectly possible for theoretical and practical insights and decisions to be reached, which are objectively right, where one would inevitably expect only errors and false steps, in view of the turbid source from which they derive. If our results really did coincide with theses based on natural law, it would merely confirm that the *polis* is in the Kingdom of Jesus Christ even when its officeholders are not aware of the fact or refuse to admit it, and therefore are unable to use the insight into the nature of the *polis* which this fact suggests. Why should it be impossible that, in spite of the State's blindness, objectively correct insights have been and are being reached again and again? The pagan State lives because such leadership of the blind has repeatedly made its stability and its functions possible. All the more reason, surely, why the Church cannot and must not withhold its witness to an insight based on clearly defined and consistently applicable facts.

XXIX

A further comment on the constancy and continuity of the Christian approach in politics: it may be remarked (again, with pleasure or annoyance) that the Christian line that follows from the gospel betrays a striking tendency to the side of what is generally called the "democratic" State. Here again, we shall be careful not to deny an obvious fact, though "democracy" in any technical meaning of the word (Swiss, American, French, etc.), is certainly not necessarily the form of State closest to the Christian view. Such a State may equally well assume the form of a monarchy or an aristocracy, and occasionally even that of a dictatorship. Conversely, no democracy as such is protected from failing in many or all of the points we have enumerated and degenerating not only into anarchy but also into tyranny and thereby becoming a bad State. It must be admitted that the word and the concept "democracy" ("the rule of the people") are powerless to describe even approximately the kind of State which, in the Christian view, most nearly corresponds to the divine ordinance. This is no reason, however, why it should be overlooked or denied that Christian choices and purposes in politics tend on the whole towards the form of State, which, if it is not actually realised in the so-called "democracies," is at any rate more or less honestly clearly intended and desired. Taking everything into account, it must be said that the Christian view shows a stronger trend in this direction than in any other. There certainly is an affinity between the Christian community and the civil communities of the free peoples.

XXX

In conclusion, we propose to discuss the problem of how Christian decisions in the political sphere may be put into action.

The first method that suggests itself is the formation and activity of a special Christian party. This has long been adopted in Holland and later in Switzerland (Evangelical People's Party), and in recent times especially in France (Mouvement Républicain Populaire) and Germany (Christian Democratic Union). On the Protestant side it has been deemed possible and necessary to join forces with Roman Catholic fellow citizens with the same political views. But parties are one of the most questionable phenomena in political life: they are in no sense its constitutive elements, and it is possible that from the very outset they have been pathological or at least no more than secondary phenomena. I wonder if the Christian community is well advised to add one more to the number of these organisations in order to fulfil its own share of political responsibility? Can there be any other "Christian" party in the State but the Christian fellowship itself, with its special mission and purpose? And if what we want is a political corollary of the Church in political life, can anything else be permissible and possible

but—please do not be scared!—a single State party excluding all others, whose programme would necessarily coincide with the tasks of the State itself, understood in the
widest sense (but excluding all particularist ideas and interests)? How can there be a special Christian party along-
side other political parties?—a party to which some Christians belong, whilst others do not—a party opposed by other
non-Christian parties (which it must nevertheless recognise
as legitimately non-Christian)? To institute special Christian parties implies that the Christian community as such
has no claim on the support of all its members for its own
political line. It implies that it cannot help but allow the
non-Christians in the State to consolidate themselves in a
non-Christian bloc in order to enforce their own anti-
Christian line. The Church's supreme interest must be rather
that Christians shall not mass together in a special party,
since their task is to defend and proclaim, in decisions based
on it, the Christian gospel that concerns all men. They must
show that although they go their own special way, they are
not in fact against anybody but unconditionally for all men,
for the common cause of the whole State.

In the political sphere the Christian community can draw
attention to its gospel only indirectly, as reflected in its political decisions, and these decisions can be made intelligible
and brought to victory not because they are based on Christian premises but only because they are politically better
and more calculated to preserve and develop the common
life. They can witness only to Christian truths. The claim
to be witnesses to Christian truths does not necessarily make
them such, however! Surely it will be inevitable that the
Christian qualities for which it can have no use in the political sphere will become an embarrassment to a Christian
party? And will not the aims and methods which it needs
if it is to be effective as a political party (the winning of
majorities and political strongholds, propaganda and the
benevolent toleration and even encouragement of non-
Christian or problematically Christian sympathisers and

even leaders; compromises and coalitions with "non-Christian" parties and so on) compel it to deny the specifically Christian content of its policy or at any rate obscure rather than illuminate it? Will such a party not inevitably be compromising the Christian Church and its message all the time? In the political sphere Christians can bring in their Christianity only anonymously. They can break through this anonymity only by waging a political battle for the Church and by so doing they will inevitably bring discredit and disgrace on the Christian name. In the authentically political questions which affect the development of the civil community, Christians can only reply in the form of decisions which could be the decisions of any other citizens, and they must frankly hope that they may become the decisions of all other citizens regardless of their religious profession. How can Christians mass together in a political party at all in these circumstances? The thing is only possible—and the suspicious alliance of the Protestants with the Romans in the French M.R.P. and the German C.D.U. shows that it becomes successful only where the Kingdom of God is interpreted as a human goal founded on natural law, where an allegedly Christian law, which is in fact a mere amalgam of humanitarian philosophy and morality, is set alongside the gospel in the political sphere. When it is represented by a Christian party, the Christian community cannot be the political salt which it is its duty to be in the civil community.

XXXI

The opportunity that it is offered to fulfil this duty is simply the one that lies nearest to hand: the preaching of the whole gospel of God's grace, which as such is the whole justification of the whole man—including political man. This gospel which proclaims the King and the Kingdom that is now hidden but will one day be revealed is political from the very outset, and if it is preached to real (Christian and non-Christian) men on the basis of a right interpretation of the Scriptures it will necessarily be prophetically political. Explications and applications of its political content in an unmistakable direction will inevitably take place (whether in direct or indirect illumination of the political problems of the day) where the Christian community is gathered together in the service of this gospel. Whether this happens or not will depend on the preachers, but not only on them. It is a bad sign when Christians are frightened by "political" sermons—as if Christian preaching could be anything but political. And if it were not political, how would it show that it is the salt and the light of the world? The Christian Church that is aware of its political responsibility will demand political preaching; and it will interpret it politically even if it contains no direct reference to politics. Let the Church concentrate first, however, on seeing that the whole gospel really is preached within its own area. Then there will be no danger of the wider sphere beyond the Church not being wholesomely disturbed by it.

XXXII

The Christian community acts within the meaning and limits of its own mission and competence when it speaks, through the mouth of its presbyterial and synodal organs, in important situations in political life, by making representations to the authorities or by public proclamations. It will be careful to select, as wisely as possible, the particular situations in which it deems it right to speak, and it will have to choose its words very prudently and very definitely if it is to be heard. It must not give the impression that it never wakes from the sleep of an otherwise non-political existence until such matters as gambling or the abuse of alcohol or the desecration of the Sabbath or similar questions of a religious and ethical nature in the narrower sense are under discussion, as if such problems were not in fact only on the verge of real political life. The Church must see that it does not make a habit of coming on the scene too late, of entering the fray only when its opinions no longer involve any particular risk and can no longer exert any particular influence. It must see above all that the idea of the Church as the representative of a definitive class-conditioned outlook and morality is not allowed to gain ground, thereby confirming those who already loyally believe in this "law" and arousing the disapproval of those who are, on the contrary, unable to regard such a "law" as in any sense eternal. All this applies just as much to the Christian journalism and writing that are carried on with or even without the authority of the Church. Christian publicists and writers must place themselves honestly in the service of the gospel which is intended for all men and not devote their gifts to some Christian fad or another.

XXXIII

Perhaps the most important contribution the Church can make is to bear in mind in the shaping of its own life that, gathered as it is directly and consciously around the common centre, it has to represent the inner within the outer circle. The real Church must be the model and prototype of the real State. The Church must set an example so that by its very existence it may be a source of renewal for the State and the power by which the State is preserved. The Church's preaching of the gospel would be in vain if its own existence, constitution, order, government, and administration were not a practical demonstration of the thinking and acting from the gospel which takes place in this inner circle. How can the world believe the gospel of the King and His Kingdom if by its own actions and attitudes the Church shows that it has no intention of basing its own internal policy on the gospel? How can a reformation of the whole people be brought about if it is common knowledge that the Church itself is bent only on self-preservation and restoration—or not even that? Of the political implications of theology which we have enumerated, there are few which do not merit attention first of all in the life and development of the Church itself. So far they have not received anything like enough attention within the Church's own borders.

What nonsense it is, for example, that in a country like Germany which has diligently to learn the rudiments of law, freedom, responsibility, equality, and so on, that is, the elements of the democratic way of life, the Church considers it necessary to act more and more hieratically and bureaucratically and becomes a refuge for nationalism in a situation in which it ought supremely to appear as the holy catholic Church, and thereby help to lead German politics out of an old defile. The Church must not forget that what it is rather than what it says will be best understood, not least in the State.

XXXIV

If the Church is a Christian community it will not need a Christian party. If it is a true fellowship it will perform with its words and its whole existence all the functions which the disastrous enterprise of "Christian" parties is evidently intended to fulfil. There will be no lack of individual Christians who will enter the political arena anonymously, that is, in the only way they can appear on the political scene, and who will act in accordance with the Christian approach and will thereby prove themselves unassuming witnesses of the Gospel of Christ, which can alone bring salvation in the political sphere no less than elsewhere. Any fame that they acquire will not be founded on the fact that they are "nice, pious people" but simply that from their own distinctive point of view they will know better than others what is best for the civil community. It is not the presence and co-operation of "Christian personalities" that helps the State. One thinks of Bismarck again: assuming for the moment that he was something like the "Christian personality" that legend describes him to have been, what difference did it make to the unfortunate tendency of his politics? What help was it to poor Germany? The way Christians can help in the political sphere is by constantly giving the State an impulse in the Christian direction and freedom to develop on the Christian line. Let it not be said that there are too few of such Christians and that these few in their isolation are helpless. How much one individual can do whose heart and soul are really wrapped up in the cause! And in any case Christians are not asked to do something in their own strength, but only what they are required to do by the grace of God.

What does it matter if they are isolated and if—since there are such things as parties—they are members of different parties, that is, of one of the various "non-Christian" parties? They will take the party programme, party discipline, party victories, and party defeats in which they are involved as seriously and humorously as the cause deserves. In every party they will be against narrow party policies and stand up for the interests of the whole community. By that token they will be political men and women in the primary meaning of the word. Scattered in different places, and known or unknown to one another, in touch with one another or out of touch, they will all be together—as citizens —and will make the same distinctions and judgments, choose and desire one cause, work for one cause. Let us pray that the Church may supply the State with such Christians, such citizens, such political men and women in the primary meaning of the word! For in their existence the Church will be fulfilling its share of political responsibility in the most direct form.

XXXV

Let me remind you once again of the fifth thesis of the *Theological Declaration* of Barmen, which I have quoted from several times already: "The Bible tells us that, in accordance with a divine ordinance, the State has the task of providing for law and peace in the world that still awaits redemption, in which the Church stands, according to the measure of human insight and human capacity, and upheld by the threat and use of force. The Church acknowledges the benefaction of this divine ordinance with a thankful, reverent heart. It reminds men of God's Kingdom, God's Commandment and justice, and thereby of the responsibility of governors and governed alike. It trusts and obeys the power of the Word by which God sustains all things."

I think that I have dealt with "The Christian Community and the Civil Community" within the terms of this thesis, and therefore in accordance with the mind of the Confessional Church in Germany. Some things would be different now if that Church had itself given more attention to this section of the Declaration in good time. But it cannot be too late to return to it now with a new seriousness, deepened and strengthened by experience.

SELECTED BIBLIOGRAPHY

(This list includes the chief writings of Karl Barth available in English, directly relevant to the questions raised in the three essays included in this volume. In every case, there is indication of the date and manner of original publication.)

THEOLOGICAL EXISTENCE TODAY! London: Hodder and Stoughton, 1933 (*Theologische Existenz heute!* Munich: Chr. Kaiser Verlag, 1933. *Theologische Existenz heute! No. I*).

TROUBLE AND PROMISE IN THE STRUGGLE OF THE CHURCH IN GERMANY. Oxford: Clarendon Press, 1938 (*Not und Verheissung im deutschen Kirchenkampf.* Bern: BEG-Verlag, 1938).

THE KNOWLEDGE OF GOD AND THE SERVICE OF GOD ACCORDING TO THE REFORMATION (Gifford Lectures). London: Hodder and Stoughton, 1938 (*Gotteserkenntnis und Gottesdienst.* Zollikon-Zurich: Evangelischer Verlag, 1938).

CHURCH AND STATE. London: S.C.M. Press, 1939 (*Rechtfertigung und Recht.* Zollikon-Zurich: Evangelischer Verlag, 1938. *Theologische Studien No. I*).

THE CHURCH AND THE POLITICAL PROBLEM OF OUR DAY. London, Hodder and Stoughton, 1939. ("Die Kirche und die politische Frage von heute" [1938], in Karl Barth, *Eine Schweizer Stimme, 1938–1945.* Zollikon-Zurich: Evangelischer Verlag, 1945.)

THIS CHRISTIAN CAUSE. New York: Macmillan, 1941. Containing: "First Letter to the French Protestants" (December 1939); "Second Letter to the French Protestants" (October 1940); and "A Letter to Great Britain from Switzerland" (April 1941). ("Ein Brief nach Frankreich" [1939]; "Eine Frage und eine Bitte an die Protestanten in Frankreich" [1940]; and "Ein Brief aus der Schweiz nach Grossbritannien" [1941]: all in Karl Barth, *Eine Schweizer Stimme, 1938–1945.* Zollikon-Zurich: Evangelischer Verlag, 1945.)

"A Letter to American Christians," *Christendom,* Vol. VIII (1943), pp. 441–58. ("Brief an einen amerkanischen Kirchenmann" [1942], in Karl Barth, *Eine Schweizer Stimme, 1938–1945.* Zollikon-Zurich: Evangelischer Verlag, 1945.)

THE ONLY WAY. New York: Philosophical Library, 1947. Containing: "How Can the Germans Be Cured?"; "Letters"; "The Germans and Ourselves." (*Wie können die Deutschen gesund werden?* Zollikon-Zurich: Evangelischer Verlag, 1945, and in *Eine Schweizer Stimme, 1938–1945.* Zollikon-Zurich: Evangelischer Verlag, 1945; "Zwei Briefwechsel" [April, 1945], in *Eine Schweizer Stimme, 1938–1945.* Zollikon-Zurich: Evangelischer Verlag, 1945; *Die Deutschen und Wir.* Zollikon-Zurich: Evangelischer Verlag, 1945, and in *Eine Schweizer Stimme, 1938–1945.* Zollikon-Zurich: Evangelischer Verlag, 1945.)

AGAINST THE STREAM: SHORTER POST-WAR WRITINGS, 1946–1952. New York: Philosophical Library, 1954. Containing (among others): "The Christian Community and the Civil Community"; "The Christian Community in the Midst of Political Change: Documents of an Hungarian Journey"; "The Church Between East and West"; "Political Decisions in the Unity of Faith"; and "The Christian Message in Europe Today." (*Christengemeinde und Bürgergemeinde.* Zollikon-Zurich: Evangelischer Verlag, 1946; *Christliche Gemeinde im Wechsel der Staatsordnungen: Dokumente einer*